Dear Teacher:

What's a Foldable?

IN THIS BOOK you will find instructions for making Foldables as well as ideas on how to use them. A Foldable is a 3-D, interactive graphic organizer. Making a Foldable gives students a fun, hands-on activity that helps them organize and retain information.

I first began inventing, designing, and adapting Foldables over thirty years ago. Today, I present Foldable workshops and keynote addresses to over fifty thousand teachers and parents a year. Students of all ages are using Foldables for daily work, note-taking activities, student-directed projects, as forms of alternative assessment, social studies journals, graphs, charts, tables, and more. You may have seen at least one of the Foldables featured in this book used in supplemental programs or staff-development workshops.

After workshop presentations, participants would often ask me for lists of activities to be used with the Foldables they had just learned to make. They needed help visualizing how Foldables could be used to display the data associated with their disciplines—in this case, Social Studies. So, over fifteen years ago, I started collecting and sharing my ideas about how Foldables could be used to meet the needs of the Social Studies teacher.

This book is the fruit of those years. It is organized in three parts. The first part introduces Foldables, explaining how they work and some of the ways they can be used. The second part gives step-by-step instructions on how to make 32 basic Foldable activities, along with practical, classroom-tested tips. Finally, the third part of the book presents suggestions for using Foldables with specific Social Studies topics.

Add and Amend

My lists are by no means meant to be exhaustive. Indeed, since I began compiling these lists over fifteen years ago, there have been many changes to the Social Studies curriculum. I have tried to keep my lists up-to-date, but history has a way of marching on, heedless of the demands of writers and publishers. That's why I've left spaces throughout the book for you to add your own ideas and activities, record new information, and amend my lists as you see fit.

I now hand these lists of ideas and information over to you and your students. Have fun using, adding to, and amending them.

Dinah Zike

Table of Contents

Introduction to Foldables

A Foldable is a 3-D, interactive graphic organizer. It can be a valuable learning tool, helping students to organize, learn, review, and remember information. In addition, using Foldables encourages student creativity, provides a means to reach kinesthetic learners, and reinforces important thinking and communication skills.

In the pages that follow, I give a brief introduction to Foldables. I have divided this section into four parts. They are:

- *Why Use Foldables in Social Studies?*
  Explains how Foldables can be used effectively for teaching Social Studies.

- *Using Social Studies Foldables to Build Communication Skills*
  Lists ways that Foldables support important reading, thinking, and communication skills that are enunciated in the National Social Studies Standards.

- *Foldable Basics*
  Offers some general tips on creating and storing Foldables and managing their use in the classroom.

- *Selecting the Appropriate Foldable*
  Gives four tables that help you to select the right Foldable for the Social Studies topic you want to cover or the skill you want to reinforce. The first three tables show how specific Social Studies topics and skills divide themselves neatly into parts. The fourth table, *Matching Part Divisions to the Correct Foldable*, shows which Foldables are best to use when dividing a topic into a specific number of parts.

 Use this table as a handy reference tool. You can refer to it often when you are deciding which foldable to use with the topics shown on pages 55–133.

Why Use Foldables in Social Studies?

When teachers ask me why they should take time to use the Foldables featured in this book, I explain that Foldables:

- quickly organize, display, and arrange data, making it easier for students to grasp Social Studies concepts, theories, facts, opinions, questions, research, and ideas.

- integrate language arts, the sciences, and mathematics into the study of Social Studies.

- incorporate the use of such skills as comparing and contrasting, recognizing cause and effect, and finding similarities and differences into daily work and long-term projects.

- can be used by students or teachers to easily communicate data through graphs, tables, charts, models, and diagrams, including Venn diagrams.

- replace teacher-generated writing or photocopied sheets with student-generated print.

- provide a multitude of creative formats in which students can present projects, research, interviews, and inquiry-based reports instead of typical poster board or Social Studies fair formats.

- result in student-made study guides that are compiled as students listen for main ideas, read for main ideas, or conduct research.

- can be used as alternative assessment tools by teachers to evaluate student progress or by students to evaluate their own progress.

- boost student feelings of ownership and investment in the Social Studies curriculum.

- offer useful tools for students to review Social Studies, vocabulary, concepts, information, generalizations, ideas, and theories, providing them with a strong foundation that they can build upon with new observations, concepts, and knowledge.

- allow students to make their own journals for recording observations, research information, primary and secondary source data, surveys, and more.

Using Social Studies Foldables to Build Communication Skills

Communication skills are important to Social Studies. Not all students will become politicians, geographers, or historians, but all students need to be able to think, analyze, and communicate using Social Studies skills. Throughout their lives, students will be called upon to be literate in the social sciences. They will need to note biases, differentiate between fact and opinion, participate in civic organizations, discuss pros and cons of actions and reactions, investigate primary and secondary sources, justify voting for or against an issue, research a topic related to their well-being or interests, make cause-and-effect decisions about their actions, write editorials to express their views publicly, and more. Foldables are one of many techniques that can be used to integrate reading, writing, thinking, debating, researching, and other communication skills into an interdisciplinary Social Studies curriculum.

Visual Skills That Organize Data
draw diagrams

develop Venn diagrams

make time lines

develop flow charts

design and use charts and/or tables

develop bar, circle, or line graphs

make concept maps or network trees

Writing Skills
list

outline

write a critique

write a summary

write an editorial

record empirical data

write interview questions

narrative writing

descriptive writing

expository writing

persuasive writing

Social Studies Skills
infer

inquire

identify

question

interview

investigate

collect data

interpret data

use primary sources

use secondary sources

Oral Language Skills
relate	describe
debate	review
explain	question
discuss	summarize
critique	

Creative Skills
design	make a mobile
diagram	make a diorama
interview	illustrate and label
make a model	complete a project

Research Skills
inquire	determine
discover	investigate
question	search the Internet
research	

Reading/Thinking Skills
note biases

read for main idea

find pros and cons

compare and contrast

determine cause and effect

Know/Want to know/Learned

find similarities and differences

differentiate between fact and opinion

Foldable Basics

What to Write and Where

Students should use the front tabs of their Foldables to write general information—titles, vocabulary words, concepts, questions, main ideas, and dates. General information is viewed every time a student looks at a Foldable. Foldables help students focus on and remember key points without being distracted by other print.

Have students write specific information—supporting ideas, student thoughts, answers to questions, research information, empirical data, class notes, observations, and definitions—under the tabs.

As you teach, demonstrate different ways in which Foldables can be used. Soon you will find that students make their own Foldables and use them independently for study guides and projects.

With Tabs or Without Tabs

Foldables with flaps or tabs create study guides that students can use to self-check what they know about the general information on the front of tabs. Use Foldables without tabs for assessment purposes (where it's too late to self-check) or projects where information is presented for others to view quickly.

With Tabs:
Venn diagram used as a study guide

Without Tabs:
Venn diagram used for assessment

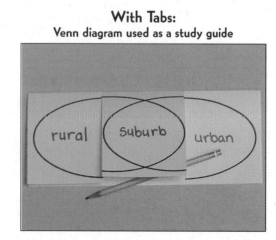

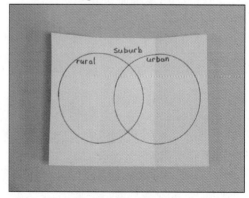

What to Do with Scissors and Glue

If it is difficult for your elementary students to keep glue and scissors at their desks, then set up a small table in the classroom and provide several containers of glue, numerous pairs of scissors (sometimes tied to the table), containers of crayons and colored pencils, a stapler, clear tape, and anything else you think students might need to make their Foldables. Don't be surprised if students donate colored markers, decorative-edged scissors, gel pens, stencils, and other art items to your publishing table.

The more they make and use Foldable graphic organizers, the faster students become at producing them.

Storing Graphic Organizers in Student Portfolios

Turn one-gallon freezer bags into student portfolios which can be collected and stored in the classroom. Students can also carry their portfolios in their notebooks if they place strips of two-inch clear tape along one side and punch three holes through the taped edge.

Have each student write his or her name along the top of the plastic portfolio with a permanent marker and cover the writing with two-inch clear tape to keep it from wearing off. Then cut the bottom corners off the bag so it won't hold air and will stack and store easily.

 I found it more convenient to keep student portfolios in my classroom so student work was always available when needed and not "left at home" or "in the car." Giant laundry-soap boxes make good storage containers for portfolios.

Let Students Use This Book as an Idea Reference

Make this book of lists available to students to use as an idea reference for projects, discussions, Social Studies debates, extra credit work, cooperative learning group presentations, and more. Soon they will be generating their own ideas for making and using Foldables.

Selecting the Appropriate Foldable

Dividing Social Studies Concepts into Parts

Foldables divide information and make it visual. In order to select the appropriate Foldable, decide how many parts you want to divide the information into and then determine which Foldable best illustrates or fits those parts..

Below are tables of typical Social Studies topics. The first table shows topoics that divide naturally into parts. The second table shows topics that can be divided into parts.

Social Studies Concepts Already Divided into Parts

General Social Stu0dies		United States History		World History	
Concept	Parts	Concept	Parts	Concept	Parts
Family and Friends	2	Maya, Aztec, Inca	3	Nomadic Cultures and Farming Cultures	2
Needs and Wants	2	Colonies	13	Tigris and Euphrates Rivers	2
Goods and Services	2	Checks and Balances	2	Upper and Lower Egypt	2
Production and Distribution	2	Local, State, Federal	3	Conquerors and the Conquered	2
Imports and Exports	2	First 10 Amendments	10	Water, Land, Air Exploration	3
City, State, Nation	3	Two-Party System of Government	2	American Revolution and French Revolution	2
Urban, Rural, Suburban	3	America Before, During, and After the Civil War	3	World War I and World War II	2
Reduce, Reuse, Recycle, Refuse	4	Ellis Island and Angel Island	2	City Country, Continent	2
Primary and Secondary Sources	2	Civil Rights and Equal Rights	2	World Population by Continent	6

Social Studies Concepts That Can Be Divided into Parts

General Social Studies	United States History	World History
Different Types of Homes	Native American Groups	Ancient Civilizations
Importance of Natural Resources	Battles of the Revolutionary War	Kingdoms of Egypt
Importance of Symbols	Important Documents	Asian Civilizations
Holidays and Culture	The Constitution	The Middle Ages
A Community Study	Local, National, and State Laws	The Renaissance
Geography of Earth's Continents	Industrial Revolution	History of Exploration
Transportation: Past and Present	Causes and Effects of the Cold War	Development of Slave Trade
The History of Communication	Equal Rights Movement	Immigration and Migration
Technology Through the Ages	United States Wars	Effects of Climate on Culture

Dividing Skills and Foldables into Parts

Foldables are a great way to reinforce reading, writing, and thinking skills. The first table below shows examples of how skills and activities can be divided into parts. The second table gives a guide for choosing which Foldable best corresponds to the way you want to organize and divide the information. You may want to refer to this page as you select activities from the lists of Social Studies topics in the third section of this book (see pages 53–133).

Skills and Activities Divided into Parts	
One Part	*Two Parts*
Find the Main Idea	Compare and Contrast
Predict an Outcome	Cause and Effect
Narrative Writing	Similarities and Differences
Descriptive Writing	Primary and Secondary Sources
Expository Writing	Facts and Opinions
Persuasive Writing	Past and Present
Three Parts	*Four Parts*
Venn Diagrams	Who, What, When, Where
Know?-Want to Know?-Learned?	What, Where, When, Why/How
Past, Present, Future	
Beginning, Middle, End	
Any Number of Parts	
Questioning	Making and Using Tables
Flow Charts	Making and Using Graphs
Vocabulary Words	Making and Using Charts
Time Lines	Sequencing Data or Events
Concept Webs or Maps	

Matching Part Divisions to the Correct Foldable	
One Part	*Two Parts*
Half-Book	Two-Tab Book
Folded Book	Pocket Book
Three-Quarter Book	Shutter Fold
Large Matchbook	Matchbook Cut in Half
Bound Book	Concept Map with Two Tabs
Three Parts	*Four Parts*
Trifold Book	Four-Tab Book
Three-Tab Book	Standing Cube
Pyramid Book	Top-Tab Book
Layered-Look Book	Four-Door Book
Concept Map with Three Tabs	
Any Number of Parts	
Accordion Book	Circle Graph
Pop-Up Book	Concept Map Book
Sentence Strip Holder	Vocabulary Book
Folded Table, Chart, or Graph	Time Line Book
Pyramid Mobile	Bound Book
Layered-Look Book	Multiple-Pocket Books
Top-Tab Book (three or more sheets of paper)	

Folding Instructions

So how do you make a Foldable? The following pages offer step-by-step instructions—where and when to fold, where to cut, how to combine Foldables to make larger projects—for making 32 basic Foldable activities. You can use or adapt these models to make Foldables for the topics covered in the third part of this book. As you do, remember it might help to cross-reference these models with the *Matching Part Divisions to the Correct Foldable* table that appears on page 9.

The instructions begin with *Basic Foldable Shapes*. These seven basic folds are the building blocks for all Foldables. I've given them friendly names, such as "hot dog fold," that make for easy visualization.

The bulk of this section, pages 13–45, is devoted to showing you how to make 32 basic Foldables. In addition to the step-by-step instructions, there are other features you should look for: notes to tell you what types of information the Foldable can help organize, photos of completed projects to help you see what a finished product looks like, and tips to give you classroom-tested ideas for Foldable construction, storage, and more. Look for the **Tip!** symbol.

Foldables can be supplemented with any number of graphic images. *Using Visuals and Graphics with Foldables*, pages 46–52, collects a number of reproducible graphics commonly used in the Social Studies curriculum, such as tables, time lines, maps, and rain gauges. No doubt as you gain more experience using Foldables, you will start to make your own collection of reproducible graphics.

Basic Foldable Shapes

The following figures illustrate the basic folds that are referred to throughout the following section of this book.

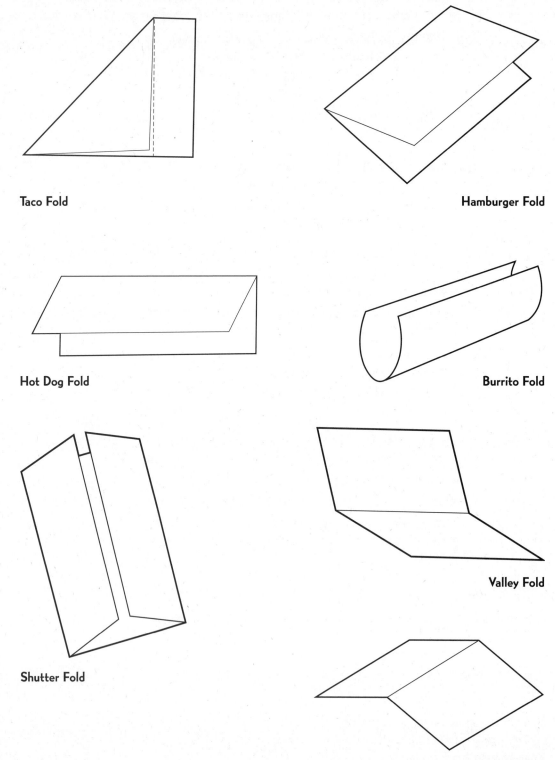

Taco Fold

Hamburger Fold

Hot Dog Fold

Burrito Fold

Shutter Fold

Valley Fold

Mountain Fold

Half-Book

Fold a sheet of paper (8 1/2" x 11") in half.

1. This book can be folded vertically like a *hot dog* or . . .

2. . . . it can be folded horizontally like a *hamburger.*

Use this book to record descriptive, expository, persuasive, or narrative writing, as well as graphs, diagrams, or charts.

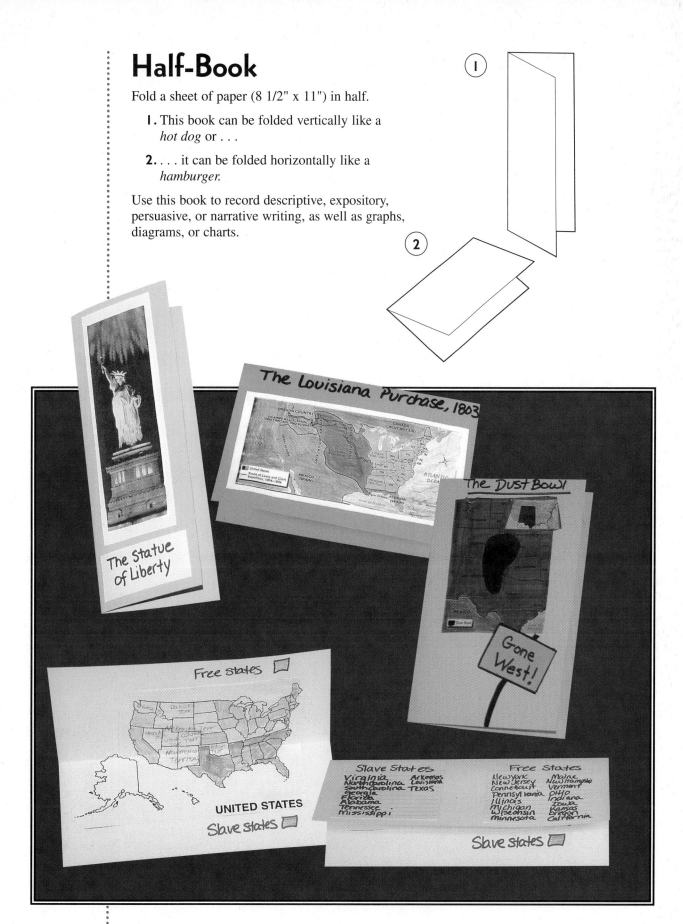

Folded Book

1. Make a *half-book* (page 13).

2. Fold it in half again like a *hamburger*. This makes a ready-made cover and two small pages inside for recording information.

Use photocopied work sheets, Internet printouts, and student-drawn diagrams or maps to make this book. One sheet of paper can be used for two activities.

Tip! **When folded, a coloring sheet becomes a book for recording notes and questions.**

Three-Quarter Book

1. Take a *two-tab book* (see page 17) and raise the left-hand tab.

2. Cut the tab off at the top fold line.

3. A larger book of information can be made by gluing several *three-quarter books* side by side.

Sketch or glue a graphic to the left, write one or more questions on the right, and record answers and information under the right tab.

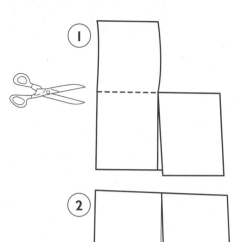

Example of several books glued side by side

Bound Book

1. Take two sheets of paper (8 1/2" x 11") and separately fold them like a *hamburger*. Place the papers on top of each other, leaving one sixteenth of an inch between the *mountain tops*.

2. Mark both folds one inch from the outer edges.

3. On one of the folded sheets, cut from the top and bottom edges to the marked spots.

4. On the second folded sheet, start at one of the marked spots and cut the fold between the two marks.

5. Take the cut sheet from step 3 and fold it like a *burrito*. Place the *burrito* through the other sheet and then open the *burrito*. Fold the bound pages in half to form an eight-page book.

Use for qualitative and quantitative observation journals. Make large project books using 11" x 17" paper.

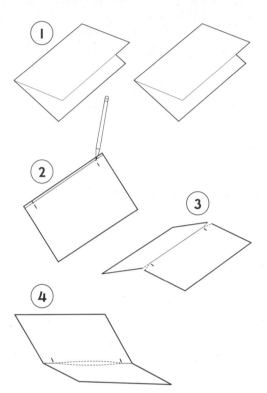

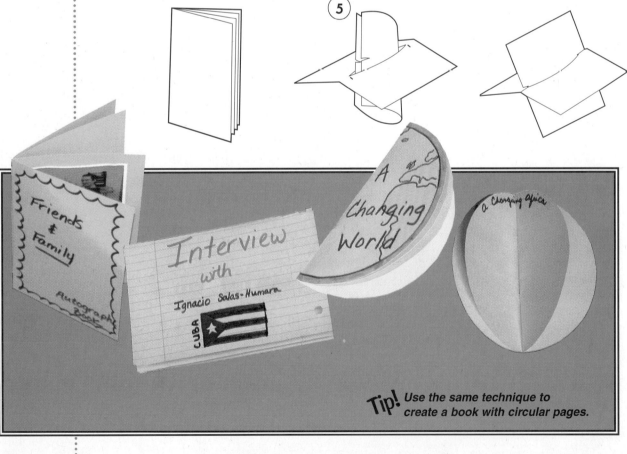

Tip! *Use the same technique to create a book with circular pages.*

Two-Tab Book

1. Take a *folded book* (see page 14) and cut up the *valley* of the inside fold toward the *mountain top*. This cut forms two large tabs that can be used front and back for writing and illustrations.

2. The book can be expanded by making several of these folds and gluing them side by side.

Use this book with data occurring in twos. For example, use it for comparing and contrasting, determining cause and effect, finding similarities and differences, and more.

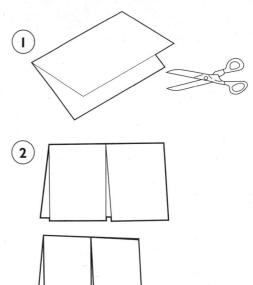

Pocket Book

1. Fold a sheet of paper (8 1/2" x 11") in half like a *hamburger*.

2. Open the folded paper and fold one of the long sides up two inches to form a pocket. Refold along the *hamburger* fold so that the newly formed pockets are on the inside.

3. Glue the outer edges of the two-inch fold with a small amount of glue.

4. **Optional:** Glue a cover around the *pocket book*.

   Variation: Make a multi-paged booklet by gluing several pockets side-by-side. Glue a cover around the multi-paged *pocket book*.

Use 3" x 5" index cards inside the pockets. Store student-made books, such as *two-tab books* and *folded books*, in the pockets.

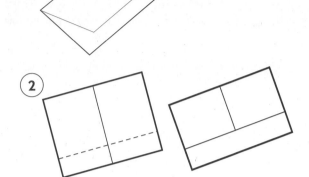

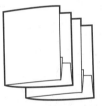

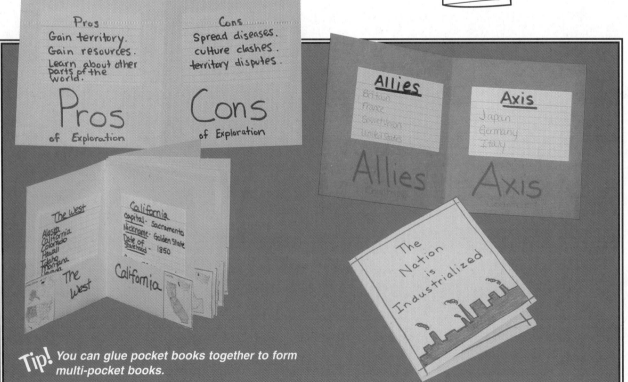

Tip! *You can glue pocket books together to form multi-pocket books.*

Matchbook

1. Fold a sheet of paper (8 1/2" x 11") like a *hamburger,* but fold it so that one side is one inch longer than the other side.

2. Fold the one-inch tab over the short side to form an envelope-like fold.

3. Cut the front flap in half toward the *mountain top* to create two flaps.

Use this book to report on one thing, such as one person, place, or thing, or for reporting on two things, such as causes and effects.

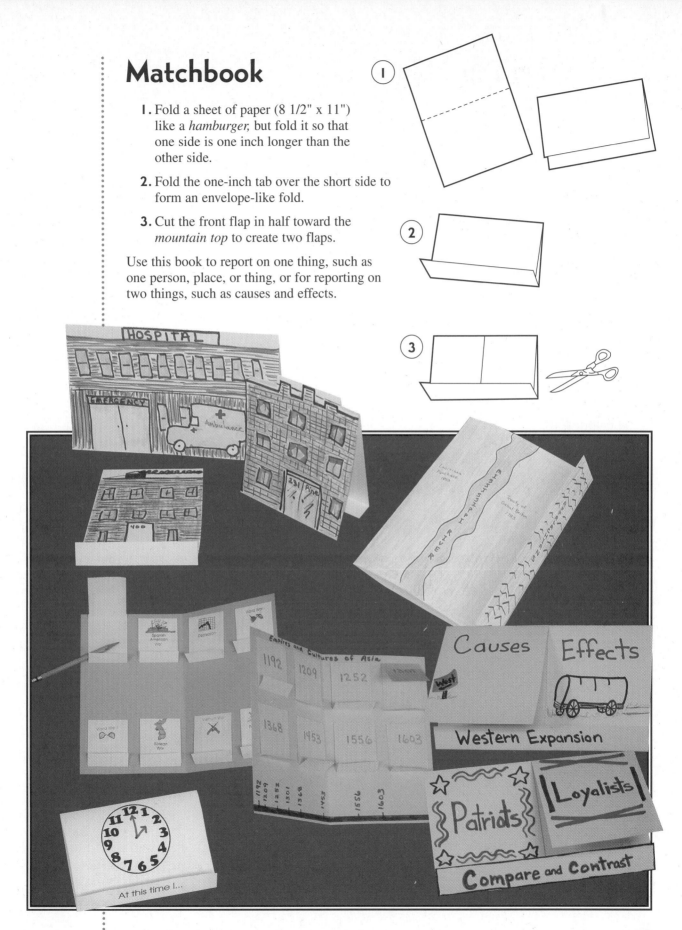

Shutter Fold

1. Begin as if you were going to make a *hamburger*, but instead of creasing the paper, pinch it to show the midpoint.

2. Fold the outer edges of the paper to meet at the pinch, or midpoint, forming a *shutter fold.*

Use this book for data occurring in twos, or make this fold using 11" x 17" paper and glue smaller books—such as the *half-book*, *journal*, and *two-tab book*—inside to create a large project full of student work.

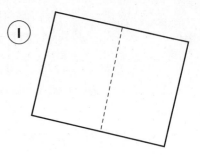

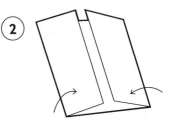

Trifold Book

1. Fold a sheet of paper (8 1/2" x 11") into thirds.

2. Use this book as is, or cut into shapes. If the trifold is cut, leave plenty of fold on both sides of the designed shape so the book will open and close in three sections.

Use this book to make charts with three columns or rows, large Venn diagrams, reports on data occurring in threes, or to show and write about the outside and inside of something.

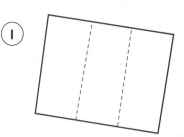

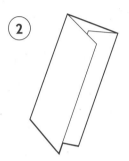

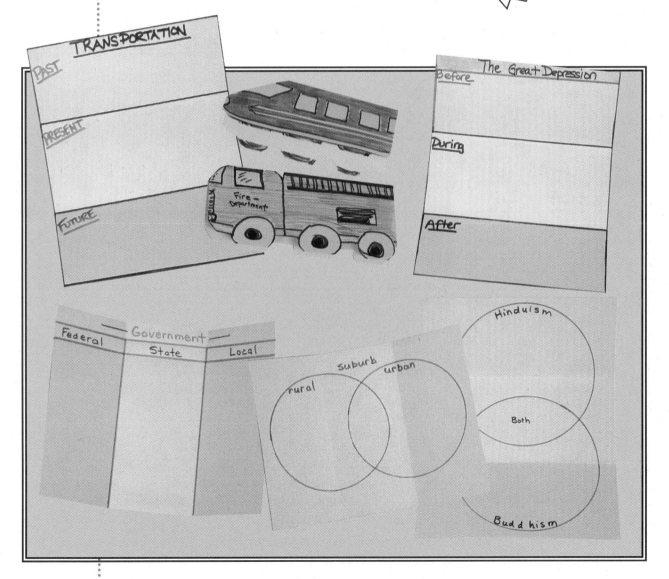

Three-Tab Book

1. Fold a sheet of paper like a *hot dog*.

2. With the paper horizontal and the fold of the *hot dog* up, fold the right side toward the center, trying to cover one half of the paper.

   NOTE: *If you fold the right edge over first, the final graphic organizer will open and close like a book.*

3. Fold the left side over the right side to make a book with three folds.

4. Open the folded book. Place one hand between the two thicknesses of paper and cut up the two *valleys* on one side only. This will create three tabs.

Use this book to record data occurring in threes or to create a two-part Venn diagram.

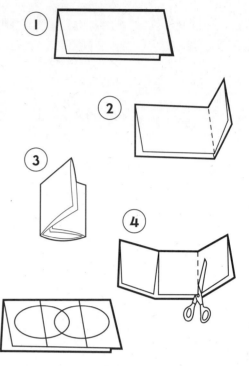

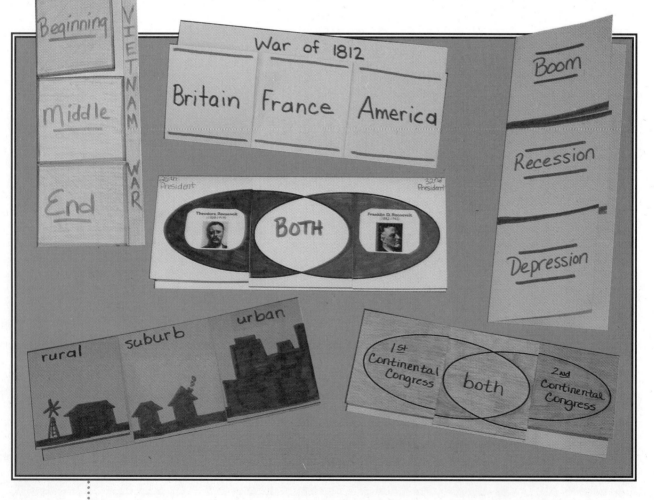

Pyramid Fold

1. Fold a sheet of paper (8 1/2" x 11") into a *taco*. Cut off the excess rectangular tab formed by the fold.

2. Open the folded *taco* and refold it like a *taco* the opposite way to create an X-fold pattern.

3. Cut one of the folds to the center of the X, or the midpoint, and stop. This forms two triangular-shaped flaps.

4. Glue one of the flaps under the other, forming a *pyramid*.

5. Label front sections and write information, notes, thoughts, and questions inside the *pyramid* on the back of the appropriate tab.

Use with data occurring in threes. Use to make mobiles and dioramas.

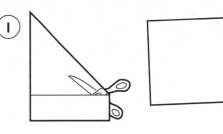

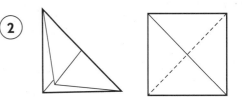

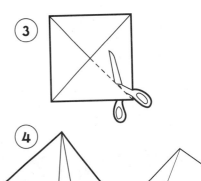

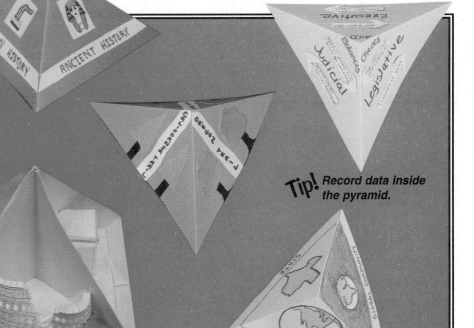

Tip! Record data inside the pyramid.

Layered-Look Book

1. Stack two sheets of paper (8 1/2" x 11") so that the back sheet is one inch higher than the front sheet.

2. Bring the bottom of both sheets upward and align the edges so that all of the layers or tabs are the same distance apart.

3. When all tabs are an equal distance apart, fold the papers and crease well.

4. Open the papers and glue them together along the *valley*, or inner center fold, or staple them along the *mountain*.

North America
Middle America
South America
The Americas

PHARAOH
GOVERNMENT OFFICIALS
SOLDIERS
SCRIBES
MERCHANTS
ARTISANS
FARMERS
SLAVES

EXCHANGE
MAP
FOOD
PLACES TO STAY
HISTORY
ACAPULCO

UNITED STATES
COLONIZATION OF MEXICO
GULF OF MEXICO
CENTRAL AMERICA
Before
During
After

WORLD
Africa
Asia
Europe
Australia
Antarctica
North America
South America

Tip! **When using more than two sheets of paper, make the tabs smaller than an inch.**

Four-Tab Book

1. Fold a sheet of paper (8 1/2" x 11") in half like a hot dog.

2. Fold this long rectangle in half like a *hamburger*.

3. Fold both ends back to touch the *mountain top* or fold it like an *accordion* (see page 31).

4. On the side with two *valleys* and one *mountain top,* make vertical cuts through one thickness of paper, forming four tabs.

Use this book for data occurring in fours. For example: community, city, state, and nation.

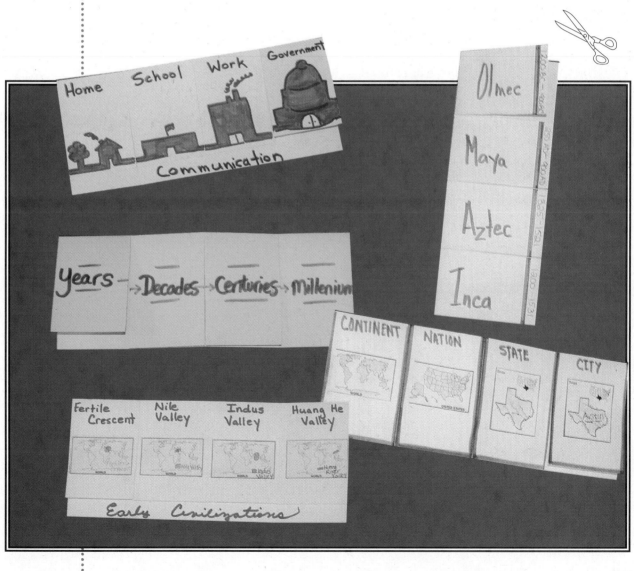

Standing Cube

1. Use two sheets of the same size paper. Fold each like a *hamburger*. However, fold one side one-half inch shorter than the other side.

2. Fold the long side over the short side on both sheets of paper, making tabs.

3. On one of the folded papers, place a small amount of glue along the the tab, next to the *valley* but not in it.

4. Place the non-folded edge of the second sheet of paper square into the *valley* and fold the glue-covered tab over this sheet of paper. Press flat until the glue holds. Repeat with the other side.

5. Allow the glue to dry completely before continuing. After the glue has dried, the cube can be collapsed flat to allow students to work at their desks. The cube can also be folded into fourths for easier storage or for moving it to a display area.

Use with data occurring in fours or make it into a project. Make a small display cube using 8 1/2" x 11" paper. Use 11" x 17" paper to make large project cubes onto which you can glue other books for display. Notebook paper, photocopied sheets, magazine pictures, and current events can also be displayed on the large cube.

Tip! *This large cube project can be stored in plastic bag portfolios.*

Envelope Fold

1. Fold a sheet of paper (8 1/2" x 11") into a *taco*. Cut off the excess paper strip.

2. Open the folded *taco* and refold it the opposite way forming another *taco* and an X-fold pattern.

3. Open the taco fold and fold the corners toward the center point of the X to create a small square envelope.

4. Trace this square on another sheet of paper. Cut and glue it to the inside of the envelope. Pictures can be placed under or on top of the tabs, or can be used to teach fractional parts.

Use this book for data occurring in fours. For younger learners, envelope folds can be used for a "hidden picture" activity. Have students select or create a picture, perhaps of current or historical events. Students can number the tabs in the order in which they are to be opened, then have a friend guess what the picture represents, raising one tab with each guess.

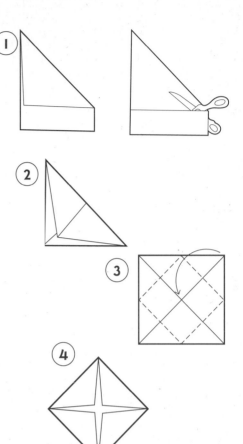

27

Four-Door Book

1. Make a *shutter fold* (see page 20) using 11" x 17" or 12" x 18" paper.

2. Fold the *shutter fold* in half like a *hamburger*. Crease well.

3. Open the project and cut along the two inside *valley* folds.

4. These cuts will form four doors on the inside of the project.

Use this fold for data occurring in fours. When folded in half like a *hamburger*, a finished *four-door book* can be glued inside a large (11" x 17") *shutter fold* (page 20) as part of a larger project.

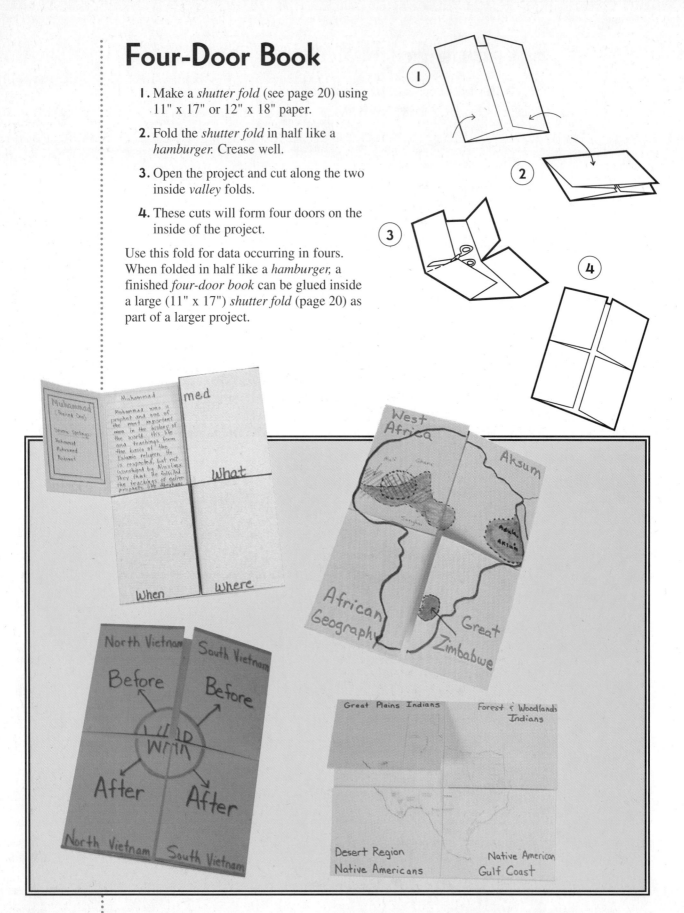

Top-Tab Book

1. Fold a sheet of paper (8 1/2" x 11") in half like a *hamburger.* Cut the center fold, forming two half sheets.

2. Fold one of the half sheets four times, each time folding in half like a *hamburger.* This folding has formed your pattern of four rows and four columns, or 16 small squares.

3. Fold two sheets of paper (8 1/2" x 11") in half like a *hamburger.* Cut the center folds, forming four half sheets.

4. Hold the pattern vertically and place a half sheet of paper under the pattern. Cut the bottom right-hand square out of both sheets. Set this first page aside.

5. Take a second half sheet of paper and place it under the pattern. Cut the first and second right-hand squares out of both sheets. Place the second page on top of the first page.

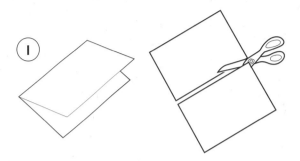

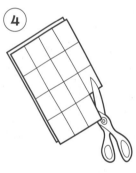

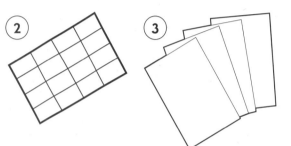

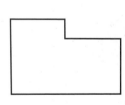

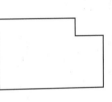

6. Take a third half sheet of paper and place it under the pattern. Cut the first, second, and third right-hand squares out of both sheets. Place this third page on top of the second page.

7. Place the fourth, uncut half sheet of paper behind the three cut-out sheets, leaving four aligned tabs across the top of the book. Staple several times on the left side. You can also glue along the left paper edges and stack them together. The glued spine is very strong.

8. Cut a final half sheet of paper with no tabs and staple along the left side to form a cover.

Tip! *Top-tabs organize information and provide more space for writing and drawing than some of the other Foldables. Use them for time lines, geographic or historic places, or sequences of events.*

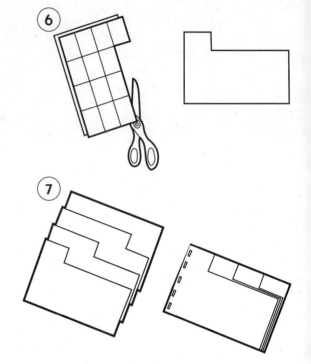

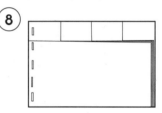

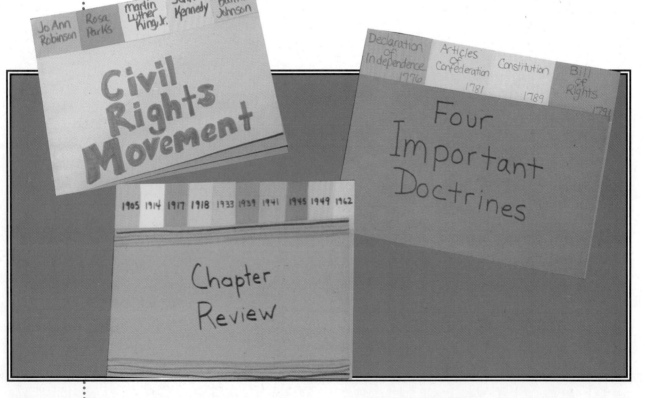

Accordion Book

1. Fold the selected paper into *hamburgers*.

2. Cut the paper in half along the fold lines.

NOTE: *Steps 1 and 2 should be done only if paper is too large to work with.*

3. Fold each section of paper into *hamburgers*. However, fold one side half an inch shorter than the other side. This will form a tab that is half an inch long.

4. Fold this tab forward over the shorter side, then fold it back away from the shorter piece of paper. (In other words, fold it the opposite way.)

5. To form an *accordion* glue a straight edge of one section into the *valley* of another section's tab.

NOTE: *Before gluing, stand the sections on end to form an* accordion. *This will help students visualize how to glue the sections together. (See illustration 5.) Always place the extra tab at the back of the book so you can add more pages later.*

Use this book for time lines, student projects that grow, sequencing events or data, and biographies.

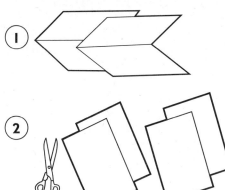

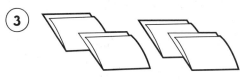

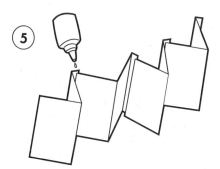

Tip! *Use different colored paper to indicate before and after, or the beginning, middle, and end of an event.*

Tip! *When folded, this project is used like a book, and it can be stored in student portfolios. When open, it makes a nice project display. Accordion books can be stored in file cabinets for future use, too.*

Pop-Up Book

1. Fold a sheet of paper (8 1/2" x 11") in half like a *hamburger.*

2. Beginning at the fold, or *mountain top,* cut one or more tabs.

3. Fold the tabs back and forth several times until there is a good fold line formed.

4. Partially open the *hamburger* fold and push the tabs through to the inside.

5. With one small dot of glue, glue figures for the *pop-up book* to the front of each tab. Allow the glue to dry before going on to the next step.

6. Make a cover for the book by folding another sheet of paper in half like a *hamburger.* Place glue around the outside edges of the *pop-up book* and firmly press inside the *hamburger* cover.

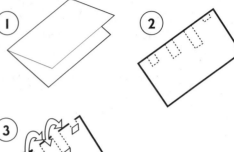

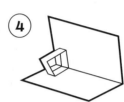

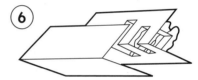

Tip! *Pop-up sheets can be glued side by side to make pop-up books.*

Tip! *Use pop-up tabs with accordion books and display boxes.*

Folding into Fifths

1. Fold a sheet of paper in half like a *hot dog* or *hamburger*.

2. Fold the paper so that one third is exposed and two thirds are covered.

3. Fold the two-thirds section in half.

4. Fold the one-third section (single thickness) backward to form a fold line.

5. Leave open for a five-part folded table or chart, or cut along each fold to create a five-tab book.

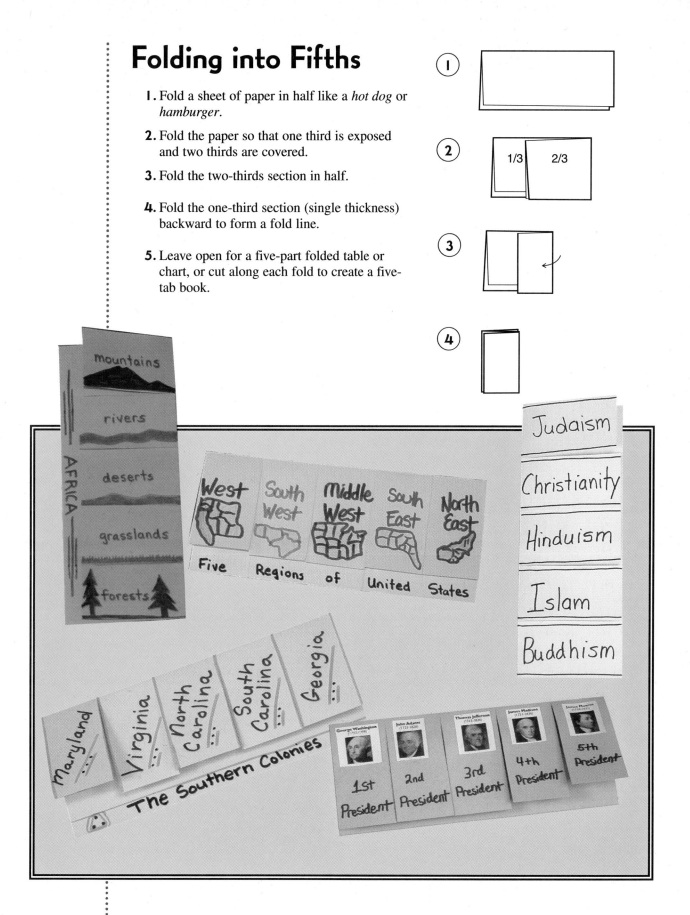

Folding a Circle into Tenths

1. Fold a paper circle in half.

2. Fold the half circle so that one third is exposed and two thirds are covered.

NOTE: *Paper squares and rectangles are folded into tenths the same way. Fold them so that one third is exposed and two thirds are covered. Continue with steps 3 and 4.*

3. Fold the one-third (single thickness) section backward to form a fold line.

4. Fold the two-thirds section in half.

5. The half circle will be divided into fifths. When opened, the circle will be divided into tenths.

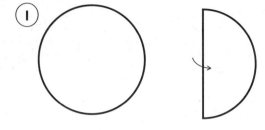

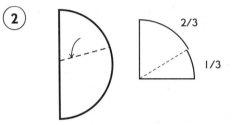

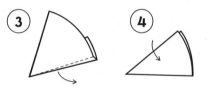

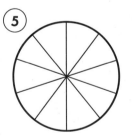

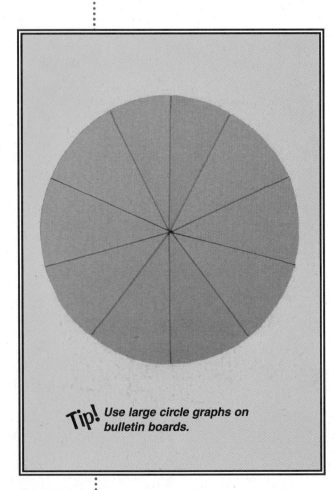

Tip! *Use large circle graphs on bulletin boards.*

Circle Graph

1. Cut out two circles using a pattern.

2. Fold each of the circles in half on each axis, forming fourths. Cut along one of the fold lines (the radius) to the middle of each circle. Flatten the circles.

3. Slip the two circles together along the cuts until they overlap completely.

4. Spin one of the circles while holding the other stationary. Estimate how much of each of the two (or you can add more) circles should be exposed to illustrate given percentages or fractional parts of data. Add circles to represent more than two percentages.

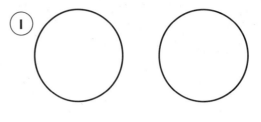

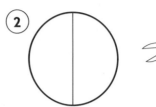

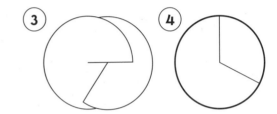

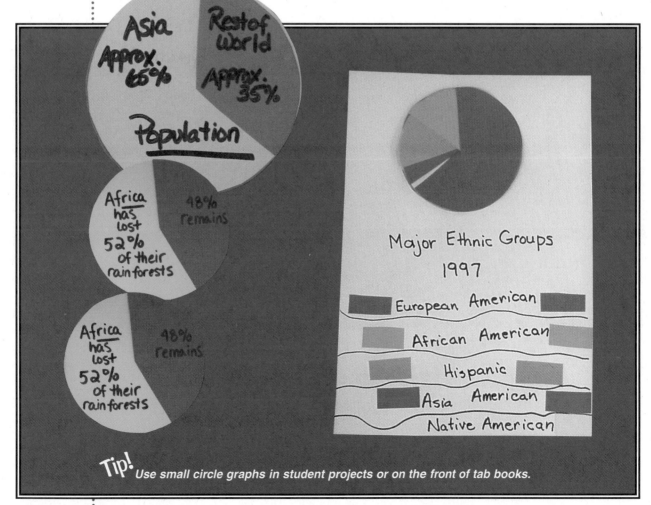

Tip! *Use small circle graphs in student projects or on the front of tab books.*

Concept Map Book

1. Fold a sheet of paper along the long or short axis, leaving a two-inch tab uncovered along the top.

2. Fold in half or in thirds.

3. Unfold and cut along the two or three inside fold lines.

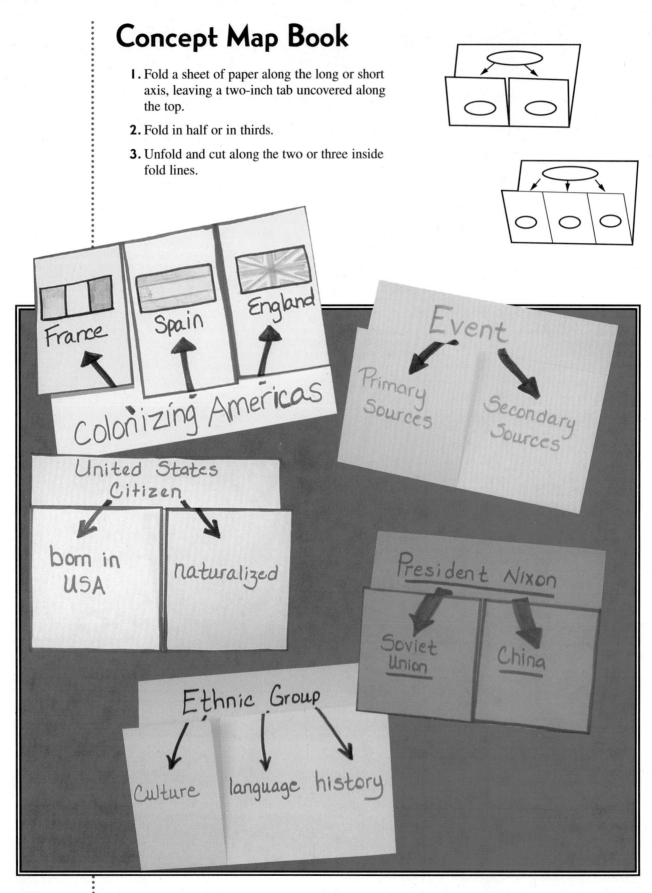

Folded Table or Chart

1. Fold the number of vertical columns needed to make the table or chart.

2. Fold the horizontal rows needed to make the table or chart.

3. Label the rows and columns.

NOTE: *Tables are organized along vertical and horizontal axes, while charts are organized along one axis, either horizontal or vertical.*

Table

Chart

	Pacific	Atlantic	Indian	Arctic
Average Depth Feet	13,740	12,254	12,740	3,407
Average Depth Meters	4,188	3,735	3,872	1,038
Deepest Point	Mariana Trench	Puerto Rico Trench	Java Trench	Eurasia Basin
Feet	36,200	28,374	25,344	17,881
Meters	11,033	8,648	7,725	5,450

School Rules	Home Rules	Play Rules	Government Rules

needs	wants
Food Clothing House	Toys Car

Plant & Animals America to Europe	Plants & Animals Europe to America

ASIA	The Ottomans	India The Moguls	The Khmer of Southeast Asia	Empires of China	Feudal Japan
country					
dynastys					
rulers					
major cities					
achievements					

Vocabulary Book

1. Fold a sheet of notebook paper in half like a *hot dog*.

2. On one side, cut every third line. This usually results in ten tabs.

3. Label the tabs.

Vocabulary books can also be used by students to take notes, record data, and write their own questions and answers.

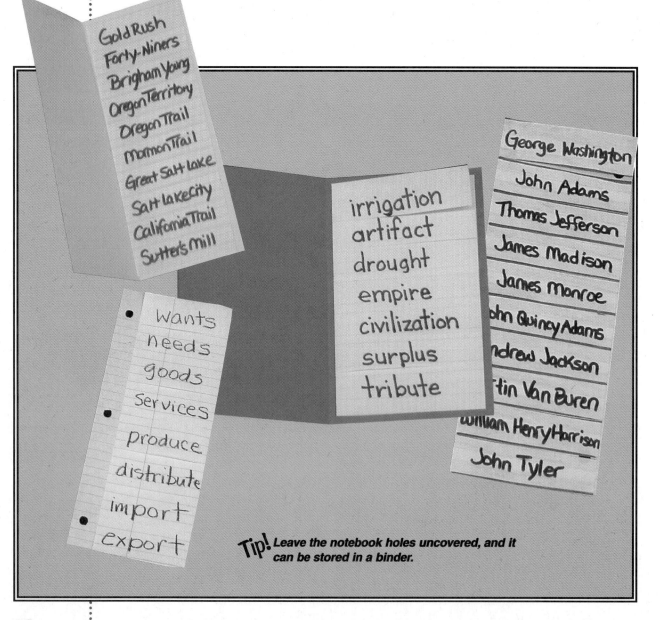

Tip! *Leave the notebook holes uncovered, and it can be stored in a binder.*

Four-Door Diorama

1. Make a four-door book out of a *shutter fold* (see page 20).

2. Fold the two inside top corners back to the outer edges (*mountains*) of the *shutter fold*. This will result in two *tacos* that will make the *four-door book* look like it has a shirt collar. Do the same thing to the bottom of the *four-door book*. When finished, four small triangular *tacos* have been made.

3. Form a 90-degree angle and overlap the folded triangles to make a diorama display that doesn't use staples or glue. (It can be collapsed for storage.)

4. If you prefer, you can cut off all four triangles or *tacos*. Staple or glue the sides to create the diorama display.

Tip! Use 11" x 17" paper to make a large diorama display case. Use poster board to make giant display cases.

Tip! Use pop-up tabs when making dioramas. Glue display cases end-to-end to sequence events or data.

Display Case

1. Make a *taco* fold and cut off the rectangular tab formed. This will result in a square.

2. Fold the square into a *shutter fold.*

3. Unfold and fold the square into another *shutter fold* perpendicular to the direction of the first. This will form a small square at each of the four corners of the sheet of paper.

4. As illustrated, cut along two fold lines on opposite sides of the large square.

5. Collapse in and glue the cut tabs to form an open box.

How to Make a Lid

Fold another open-sided box using a square of paper half an inch larger than the square used to make the first box. This will make a lid that fits snugly over the display box. Example: If the base is made out of an 8 1/2" paper square, then make the top out of a 9" square.

Cut a hole out of the lid and cover the opening with a cut piece of acetate used on overhead projectors. Heavy, clear plastic wrap or scraps from a laminating machine will also work. Secure the clear plastic sheet to the inside o the lid with glue or tape.

NOTE: *You can place polystyrene foam or quilt batting in the boxes to display insects. Glue the boxes onto a sheet of cardboard to make them strong enough to display rocks and minerals.*

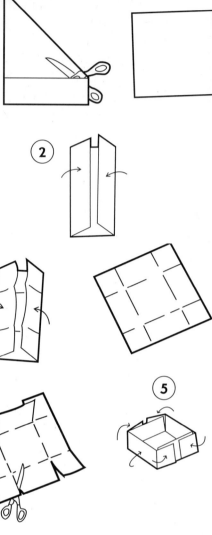

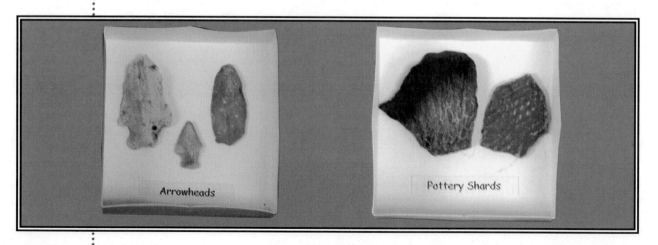

Arrowheads

Pottery Shards

Picture Frame Book

1. Fold a sheet of paper (8 1/2" x 11") in half like a *hamburger.*

2. Open the *hamburger* and gently roll one side of the *hamburger* toward the *valley.* Try not to crease the roll.

3. Cut a rectangle out of the middle of the rolled side of the paper to leave a half-inch border and form a frame.

4. Fold another sheet of paper (8 1/2" x 11") in half like a *hamburger.* Apply glue to the inside border of the picture frame and place the folded, uncut sheet of paper inside.

Use this book to feature a person, place, or thing. Inside the picture frames, glue photographs, magazine pictures, computer-generated graphs, or have students sketch pictures. This book has four inside pages for writing and recording notes.

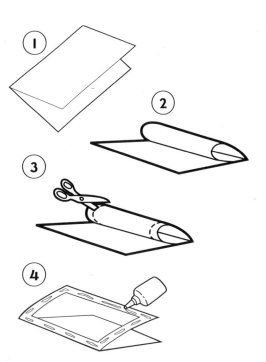

Project Board with Tabs

1. Draw a large illustration or a series of small illustrations, or write on the front of one of two pieces of selected-size paper.

2. Pinch and slightly fold the paper at the point where a tab is desired on the illustrated project board. Cut into the paper on the fold. Cut straight in, then cut up to form an "L." When the paper is unfolded, it will form a tab with an illustration on the front.

3. After all tabs have been cut, glue this front sheet onto the second piece of paper. Place glue around all four edges and in the middle, away from tabs.

4. Write or draw under the tabs.

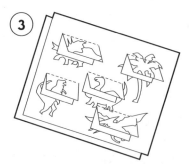

Tip! *If the project is made as a bulletin board using butcher paper, quarter and half sheets of paper can be glued under the tabs.*

Billboard Project

1. Fold all pieces of the same size of paper in half like *hamburgers*.

2. Place a line of glue at the top and bottom of one side of each folded billboard section and glue them edge-to-edge on a background paper or project board. If glued correctly, all doors will open from right to left.

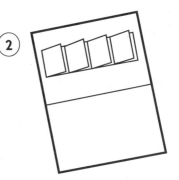

3. Pictures, dates, words, etc., go on the front of each billboard section. When opened, writing or drawings can be seen on the inside left of each section. The base, or the part glued to the background, is perfect for more in-depth information or definitions.

Use for timelines or sequencing data, such as events in a war, Presidents of the United States, or ratification of states.

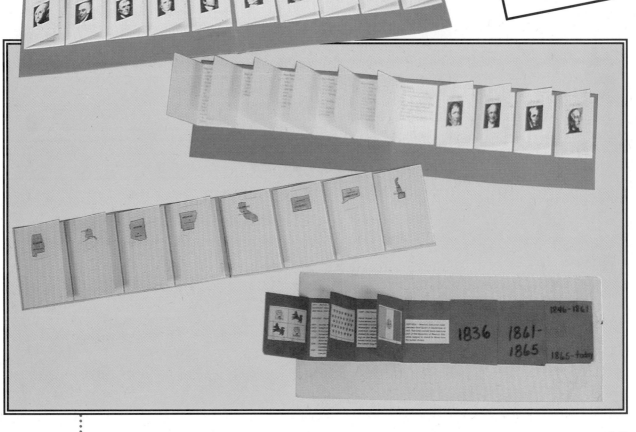

Sentence Strips

1. Take two sheets of paper (8 1/2" x 11") and fold into *hamburgers*. Cut along the fold lines making four half sheets. (Use as many half sheets as necessary for additional pages to your book.)

2. Fold each sheet in half like a *hot dog*.

3. Place the folds side by side and staple them together on the left side.

4. One inch from the stapled edge, cut the front page of each folded section up to the mountain top. These cuts form flaps that can be raised and lowered.

NOTE: *To make a half cover, use a sheet of construction paper one inch longer than the book. Glue the back of the last sheet to the construction paper strip, leaving one inch on the left side to fold over and cover the original staples. Staple this half cover in place.*

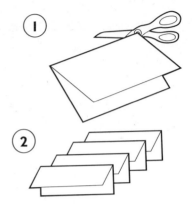

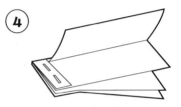

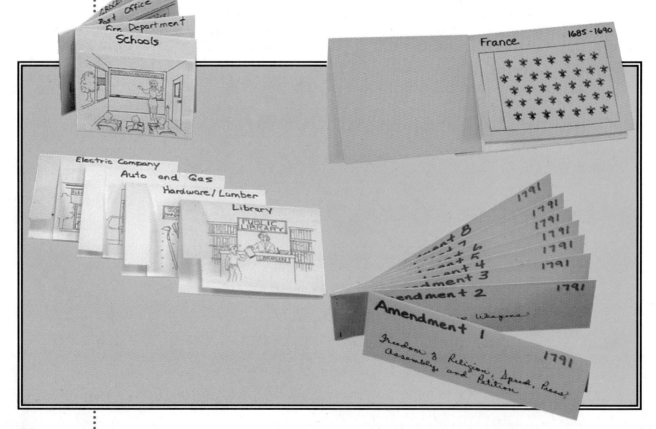

Sentence Strip Holder

1. Fold a sheet of paper (8 1/2" x 11") in half like a *hamburger*.

2. Open the *hamburger* and fold the two outer edges toward the *valley*. This forms a *shutter fold*.

3. Fold one of the inside edges of the *shutter* back to the outside fold. This fold forms a floppy "L."

4. Glue the floppy L-tab down to the base so that it forms a strong, straight L-tab.

5. Glue the other shutter side to the front of this L-tab. This forms a *tent* that is the backboard for the flashcards or student work to be displayed.

6. Fold the edge of the L-tab up one quarter to one half to form a lip that will keep the student work from slipping off the holder.

Glue down

Tip! *Use these holders to display student work on a table, or glue them onto a bulletin board to make it interactive.*

Using Visuals and Graphics with Foldables

I designed the graphics on pages 47–52 to be used as visual aids for student Foldable production. At the same time, they immerse students in measurement, percentages, maps, and time lines. Students can also incorporate them into their journals, notes, projects, and study guides independently.

Tip! *If you have the technological capability, consider scanning these graphics into a classroom computer, where you and students can select and print them out as needed.*

1. Mark and label large United States and world maps to show where past and recent events occurred, where a historic person lived and worked, where wars were fought and battles won, where volcanoes are active and inactive, where boundaries of territories or regions existed, etc.

2. Mark and label smaller maps of continents to illustrate more specific locations, for example, when making a "who, what, when, where" Foldable.

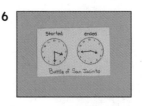

3. Hundreds grids can be used to illustrate percentages, decimals, and bar graphs.

4. Use time lines to record when someone lived or when an event or sequence of events occurred. Use two time lines to compare what was happening in two different areas at the same time.

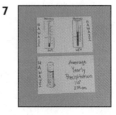

5. Use small picture frames to sketch or name a person, place, or thing. These are great to use with the four-door book as a "who, what, when, where" activity.

6. Make clocks available for students to record when something starts and stops. The clocks can be glued onto graphic organizers or observation journals. Many of the elementary students I see can't tell time unless it is digital. These graphics provide much needed practice.

7. Use rain gauges and thermometers in projects to record average precipitation amounts or average seasonal temperatures of a geographic area.

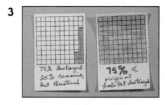

NOTE: *I grant you permission to photocopy these pages and place copies of them in the production center or publishing center of your classroom. I also grant you permission to scan these pages and use them electronically.*

Reproducible Social Studies Graphics

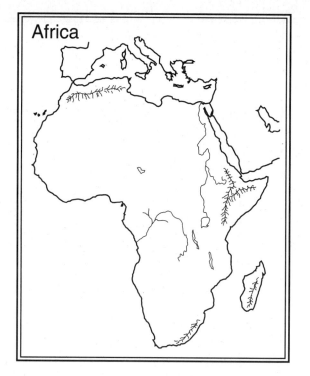

Africa

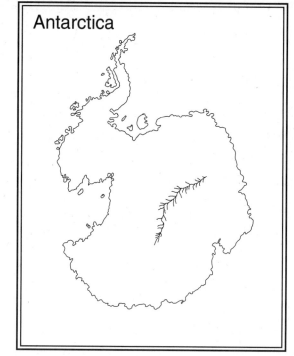

Antarctica

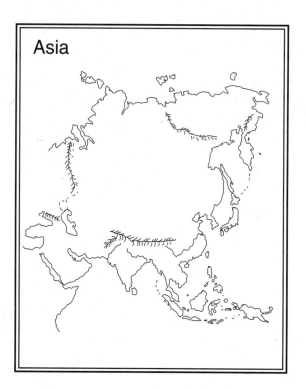

Asia

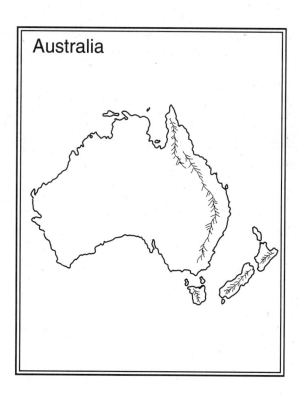

Australia

Reproducible Social Studies Graphics

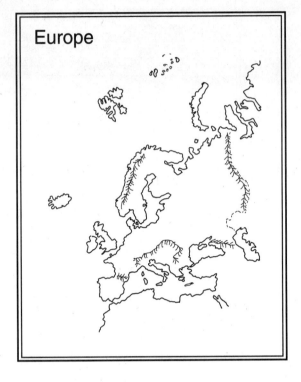

Europe

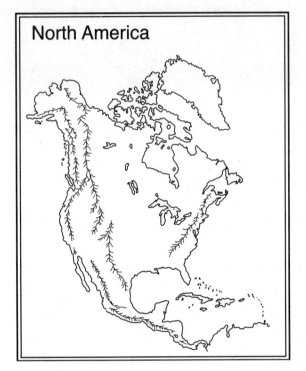

North America

South America

Picture Frame

Reproducible Social Studies Graphics

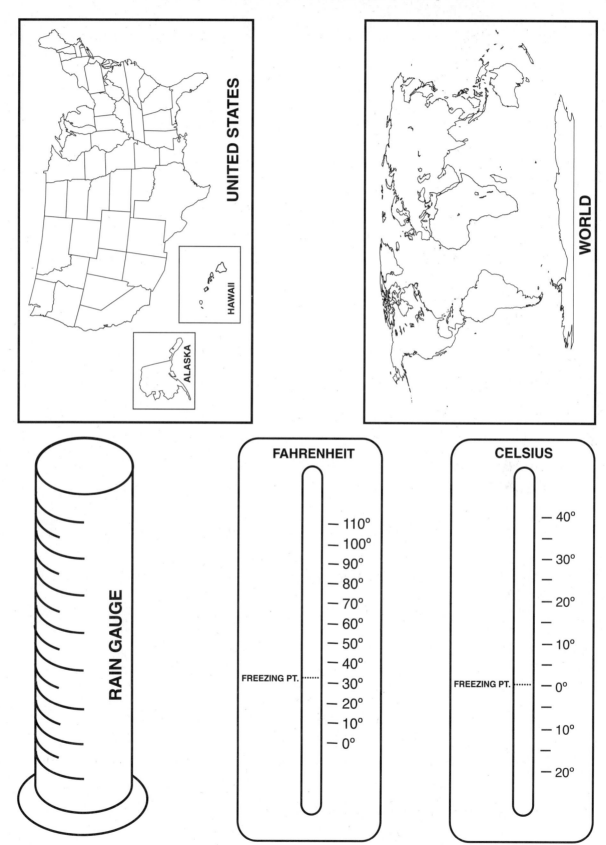

UNITED STATES

HAWAII

ALASKA

WORLD

RAIN GAUGE

FAHRENHEIT

— 110°
— 100°
— 90°
— 80°
— 70°
— 60°
— 50°
— 40°
FREEZING PT. ········· — 30°
— 20°
— 10°
— 0°

CELSIUS

— 40°
—
— 30°
—
— 20°
—
— 10°
—
FREEZING PT. ········· — 0°
—
— 10°
—
— 20°

Reproducible Social Studies Graphics

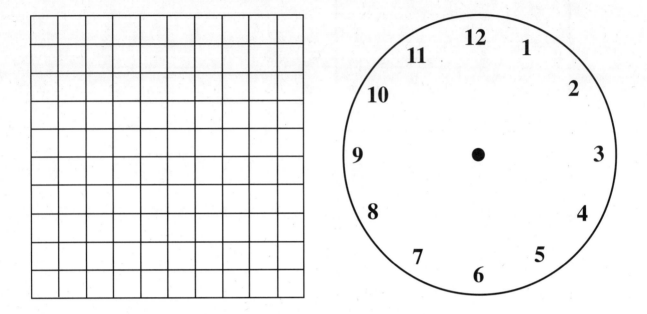

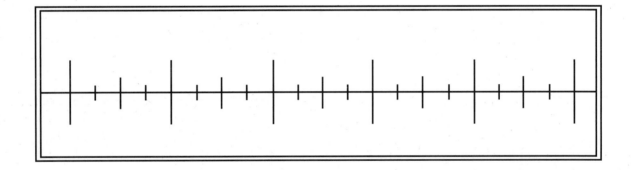

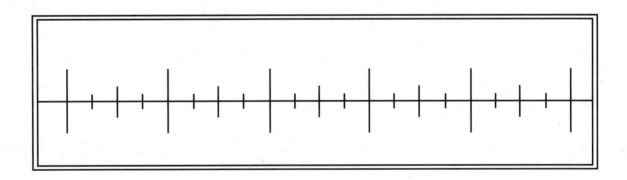

Reproducible Social Studies Graphics

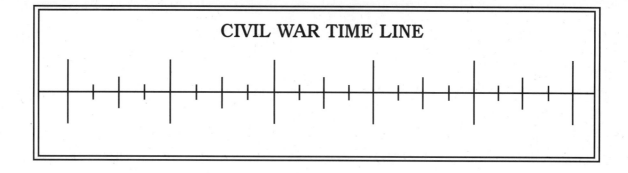

CIVIL WAR TIME LINE

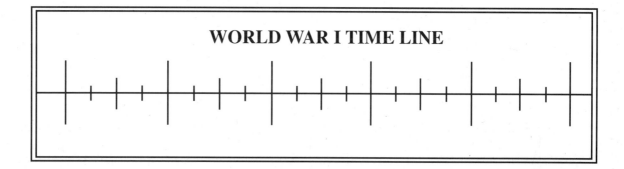

WORLD WAR I TIME LINE

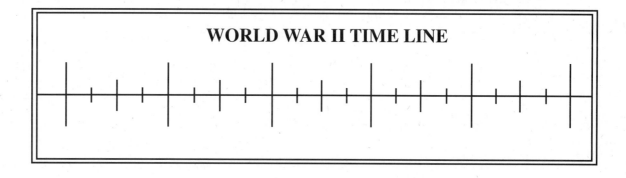

WORLD WAR II TIME LINE

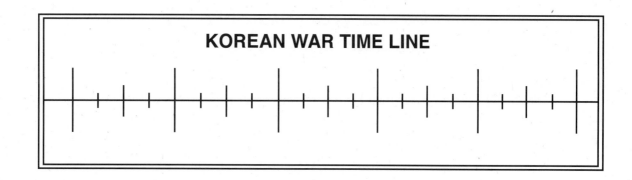

KOREAN WAR TIME LINE

Reproducible Social Studies Graphics

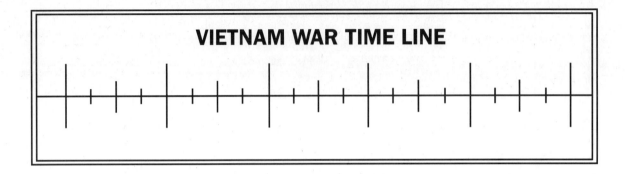

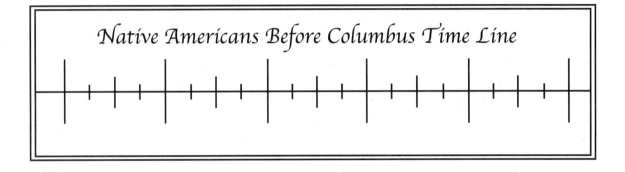

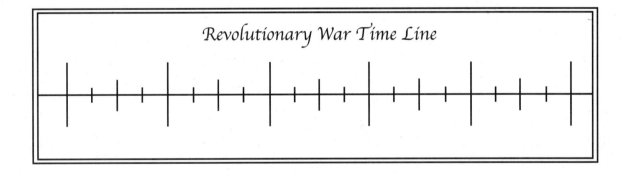

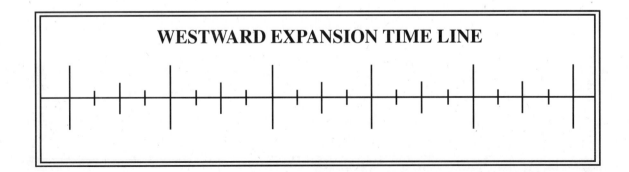

Social Studies Topic Ideas

In this section of the book, you will find lists of Social Studies topics that can be supported with Foldable activites. The topics are divided into three categories:

- **General Social Studies Topics**
  (Many of these topics are particularly suitable for Social Studies content taught in grades 1–4.)

- **United States History Topics**
  (Many of these topics are particularly suitable for Social Studies content taught in grade 5.)

- **World History Topics**
  (Many of these topics are particulary suitable for Social Studies content taught in grade 6.)

For your convenience, a table of contents precedes each category.

Under each topic you will find a list of Foldable activities you can use to augment your lesson plans. Activities are listed according to the skills or strategies that students will practice, the activity topics covered, and the suggested number of Foldable parts to use with the activity.

General Topics

The following Social Studies topics are covered in this section:

Citizenship

Skills/Strategies	Activity Suggestion	Foldable Parts
K-W-L	write about what you know, want to know, and learned about citizenship	3
Define	citizenship and nationality	2
Explain	how three or more of the following relate to citizenship: taking turns, working together, following rules, listening to others, being fair, and thinking of others' feelings and needs	3 or more
Describe	ways in which people become citizens of the United States: 1. born in the United States 2. naturalization	2
Outline	the naturalization process	any number
Research	how many people become citizens of the United States each year	1
List	examples of citizen's rights and responsibilities	2
Identify	situations in which citizens might have differing opinions and explain how citizens can voice their opinions	2
Research	four ways in which citizens can take part in their government: voting, campaigning, paying taxes, volunteering, serving in military, running for a political office, etc.	4
Debate	whether a person can or cannot be a citizen of the world	2
Differentiate between	citizens, nationals, legal aliens, and illegal aliens	4
Describe	what it means to have dual citizenship and how dual citizenship is obtained	2
Make a concept map	of expatriation, by choice and by law	2
Show cause and effect	of being stateless	2
Make a Venn diagram	of how a person can become a citizen of the United States, a citizen of Canada, or both	3
Read	the oath of allegiance taken to become a citizen of the United States	1
Make a time line	of the history of citizenship	any number

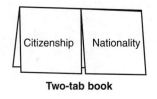

Two-tab book

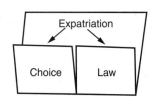

Concept map

Four-tab book

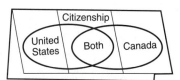

Three-tab Venn diagram

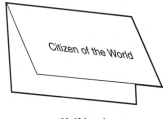

Half-book

Communication

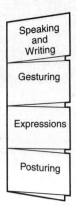

Four-tab book

Skills/Strategies	Activity Suggestion	Foldable Parts
K-W-L	write about what you know, want to know, and learned about communication	3
Define	communication	1
Describe	four ways in which people communicate: speaking and writing, gesturing, expressions, and posturing	4
Find similarities and differences	between personal communication and mass communication	2
Research	the history of writing	any number
Investigate	the development of five tools for mass communication: newspapers, pamphlets, books, telegraphs, photographs, typewriters, phonographs, telephones, radios, televisions, computers, fax machines, mobile and satellite telephones	5
Show cause and effect	of advances in communications technology and the time needed to send a message	2
Explain	ways in which people communicate at home, at school, at work, in government	4
	three ways in which communication influences culture	3
Compare and contrast	communication in ancient times, past times, and recent times	3

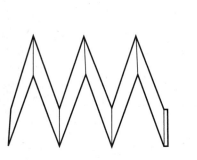

Time line:
"The History of Writing"

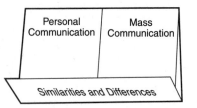

Two-tab matchbook

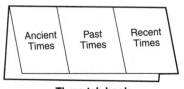

Three-tab book

Community

Skills/Strategies	Activity Suggestion	Foldable Parts
K-W-L	write about what you know, want to know, and learned about community	3
Define	community	1
Investigate	your community	any number
Describe	the people in your community	any number
Draw	examples of buildings found in your community	any number
Determine	where most of the people live in your community	1
Compare and contrast	your community's past and its present	2
	your community with another community	2
	small communities (towns) to large communities (cities)	2
Predict	the future of your community and explain your predictions	2
List	six businesses in your community	6
	jobs that require people to work during the day, during the night, and both day and night	3
Draw	two things that are unique to your community or two symbols of your community	2
Identify	four different types of jobs and workplaces in your community	4
Associate	tools, uniforms, vehicles, and buildings with workers and their jobs	any number
Make a chart	of jobs that deal with food, clothing, homes, protection, health care, etc.	5 or more
Differentiate between	urban, rural, and suburban communities	3
Make a table	of jobs, buildings, transportation, animals found in cities and on farms	any number
Describe	communities near water, in forests, mountains, and deserts	4
Explain	how a community can affect a city, nation, and other parts of the world	3
Make a Venn diagram	of a neighborhood as part of a community	2

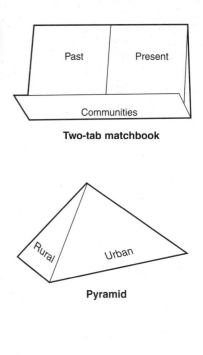

Two-tab matchbook

Pyramid

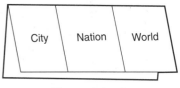

Three-tab book

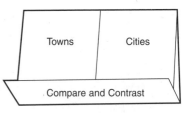

Two-tab matchbook

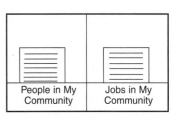

Pocket book

Country

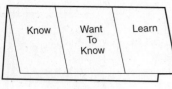

Three-tab book

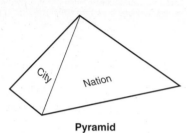

Pyramid

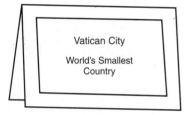

Picture frame book

World's Nine Largest Countries
Russia
Canada
China
United States
Brazil
Australia
India
Argentina
Kazakhstan

Layered book
(5 sheets of paper)

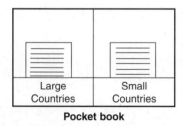

Pocket book

Skills/Strategies	Activity Suggestion	Foldable Parts
K-W-L	write about what you know, want to know, and learned about your country	3
Recognize	the United States of America on a map and on a globe	2
Find	your city, state, and country on a map	3
Refer	to the people who live in the United States of America as Americans	1
Describe	nation, state, city	3
	continent, nation, state, city	4
Draw	four symbols of your country	4
Identify	the flags of your country and your state	2
Say	the Pledge of Allegiance to the U.S. flag	1
Define	country	1
Research	how many countries there are in the world and describe three of them	3
Locate	the world's smallest country on a map or globe: Vatican City, 1/6 square mile	1
	the world's largest country on a map or globe: Russia, 6,592,850 square miles	1
Investigate	the world's nine largest countries: Russia Canada China United States Brazil Australia India Argentina Kazakhstan	9
Make a time line	of the history of a country	any number

Cultures

Skills/Strategies	Activity Suggestion	Foldable Parts
K-W-L	write about what you know, want to know, and learned about cultures	3
Define	culture as the way of life of a people	1
	ethnic group as people who share the same customs, language, and history	3
List	four things that are part of a culture: customs, beliefs, language, religion, dress, food, etc.	4
Ask	questions when learning about a culture: What language do the people speak? What clothes do they wear? What foods do they eat? What natural resources do they use? What kind of dwellings do they live in? What kind of work do they do? What kind of government do they have? How do they judge right from wrong?	any number
Describe	the United States as a country of great cultural diversity and give three examples	3
Compare and contrast	the cultures of two different ethnic groups	2
	United States culture, past and present	2
List	three things that unite the many cultures living in the United States: shared beliefs in freedoms, rights, and values	3
Research	the history of immigration to the United States	any number
Make a Venn diagram	of past reasons for immigration, present reasons for immigration, both	3
Graph	the populations of the major ethnic groups: European American, African American, Hispanic American, Asian American, Native American	5
Define	enculturation and explain how it unifies people	2
Explain	three of the characteristics of culture: 1. Culture satisfies human needs. 2. Culture is learned. 3. Culture is based on symbols and traditions.	3
Investigate	cultural traits called patterns	1

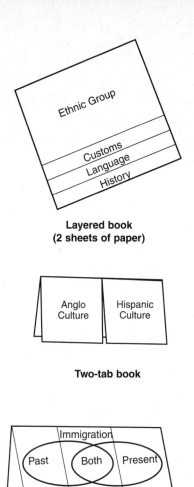

**Layered book
(2 sheets of paper)**

Two-tab book

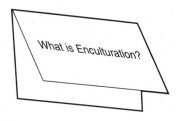

Three-tab Venn diagram

Half-book

Three-tab book

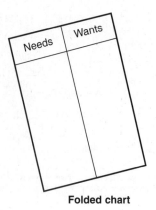

Folded chart

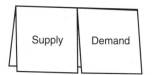

Two-tab book

Pocket book

Standing cube

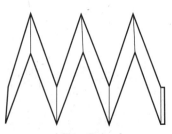

**Time line:
"The Great Depression"**

Economics

Skills/Strategies	Activity Suggestion	Foldable Parts
K-W-L	write about what you know, want to know, and learned about economics	3
Define	economics	1
List	examples of your needs and wants	2
Explain	how families help provide for our needs and wants	2
Classify	needs people can produce and needs people purchase	2
Compare and contrast	ways in which people meet their needs, past and present	2
	the wants and needs of a family and the wants and needs of a nation	4
Distinguish between	needs and wants	2
	goods and services	2
	production and distribution	2
	supply and demand	2
Describe	what happens to the cost of goods and services if the resources used to produce them are scarce	1
Investigate	the Law of Supply and the Law of Demand	2
Research	imports and exports of the United States	2
Outline	what is needed to produce goods and services: 1. natural resources 2. money 3. labor 4. technology	4
Differentiate between	booms, recessions, and depressions	3
Make a time line	of the Great Depression	any number

Exploration

Skills/Strategies	Activity Suggestion	Foldable Parts
K-W-L	write about what you know, want to know, and learned about exploration	3
Define	exploration	1
Debate	how humankind has always explored and continues to explore the world	1
Compare and contrast	methods of exploration, past and present	2
	technology used in exploration, past and present	2
Imagine	how and why prehistoric people might have been explorers	2
Describe	three of the first European explorers and their exploration goals	3
Outline	the Age of Exploration	any number
Make a Venn diagram	of Spanish Exploration, Portuguese Exploration, and both	3
Explain	reasons for European exploration: establish trade routes, to find new natural resources, spread religion, colonization	4
Draw and label	different types of ships used for exploration, such as the caravel	any number
Find	three different exploration routes on a map or globe	3
Research	two navigation tools that make exploration possible: astrolabe, magnetic compass, etc.	2
Show cause and effect	of the beginning of the Renaissance and increased interest in exploration	2
Predict	the future of exploration	1
Make a time line	of key events in the history of exploration	any number
Research	the "who, what, when, where" of Marco Polo or Prince Henry of Portugal	4

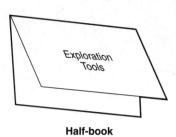

Half-book

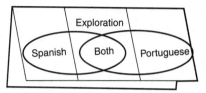

Three-tab Venn diagram

Four-tab book

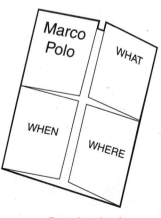

Four-door book

Family

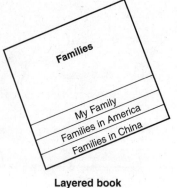

Families

My Family
Families in America
Families in China

**Layered book
(2 sheets of paper)**

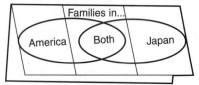

Families in...

America Both Japan

Three-tab Venn diagram

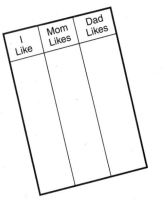

I Like | Mom Likes | Dad Likes

Folded chart

Favorites | Food | Pets | Color
Me
Mindy
Rigdon

Folded table

Pockets Full of Photographs

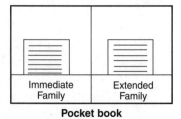

Immediate Family | Extended Family

Pocket book

Skills/Strategies	Activity Suggestion	Foldable Parts
K-W-L	write about what you know, want to know, and learned about family	3
Define	family	1
Describe	who makes up a family: parents, step-parents, children, grandparents, foster parents, brothers, sisters, aunts, uncles, cousins, etc.	any number
List	names of family members	any number
	three things families do together	3
	four basic needs of families: food, clothing, shelter, and love	4
Explain	how people can be part of a family even when they do not live together	1
Draw	pictures of your friends and family members	any number
Make a Venn diagram	of homes for one family, homes for more than one family, both	3
	families in America, families in another country, both	3
Make a table	showing the favorite things of your family members	any number
Research	the "who, what, when, where" of a family member	4
Recognize	that families differ in size and composition	2
	that families have to work together to solve problems	2
Describe	three ways in which families change: marriages; new children born or adopted; family members move; parents might separate, divorce, remarry, or die; children might move in with other relatives; etc.	3
	four kinds of homes families might live in: apartment complex, single-family home, trailer home, duplex	4
Write	the address for your family's home	1
	two thank-you notes to members of your family	2
Draw	your family in your neighborhood	2

Friends

Skills/Strategies	Activity Suggestion	Foldable Parts
K-W-L	write about what you know, want to know, and learned about friends and friendship	3
Describe	what it means to be a friend	1
List	names of friends and things friends do together	any number
Explain	three things that make someone your friend	3
	how you make new friends	1
Read	a book about friends and report on it	2
Make a concept map	on friendship	any number
Tell	ways you can be a friend to someone you know and to someone you don't know	2
Make a table	showing the favorite things of some of your friends: colors, food, clothing, TV show, animal, etc.	any number
Research	the "who, what, when, where" of a friend	4
Make a time line	outlining a friendship	any number
Make	an address book to record the addresses and/or phone numbers of your friends	1
	an autograph book to collect notes from your friends	1
Take	photographs of your friends or collect their school pictures for a friendship album	1
Investigate	famous friendships, such as the one between John Adams and Thomas Jefferson	any number

Read	stories and legends about friendship:
	   Damon and Pythias, Greek legend
	   Frog and Toad, *Frog and Toad Are Friends*, Arnold Lobel
	   Arnold and Charlotte, *Charlotte's Web*, E. B. White
		any number

Sing	"Auld Lang Syne," a song of friendship often sung on New Year's Eve	1

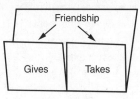

Concept map

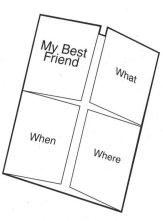

Four-door book

Bound book

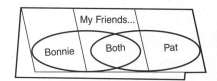

Three-tab Venn diagram

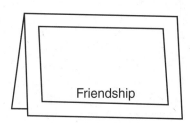

Picture frame book

Geography

The Seven Continents
North America
South America
Europe
Asia
Africa
Antarctica
Australia

Layered book
(four sheets of paper)

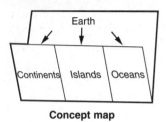

Concept map

Three-tab Venn diagram

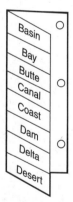

Vocabulary book

4x4 folded table

Skills/Strategies	Activity Suggestion	Foldable Parts
K-W-L	write about what you know, want to know, and learned about geography	3
Recognize	Earth as a planet in space	1
	that Earth's surface is composed of land and water	2
Describe	a globe as a model of Earth	1
Locate	continents, islands, and oceans on a map or globe	3
Name and find	the seven continents	7
	Earth's three largest islands	3
	Earth's oceans divided into smaller ocean regions	4
Define	a geographic region as a large area with common features that distinguish it from other areas	1
Investigate	three or more characteristics of a region: climate, culture, landforms, history, government	3 or more
Identify	the six regions of the United States: West, Mountain States, Middle West, Southwest, Southeast, Northeast	6
Compare and contrast	the six regions of the United States	2
Make a table	to record information on the landforms, water sources, natural resources, climate, and states of each of the six regions	any number
Make a Venn diagram	of arid climate regions (less than 20 inches of rain a year), humid climate region (over 20 inches), both	3
Define	geography terms: basin, bay, butte, canal, coast, dam, delta, desert, dune, glacier, gulf, harbor, hill, island, isthmus, lake, mesa, mountain, ocean, peninsula, plain, plateau, port, reservoir, river, strait, tributary, volcano, waterfall	any number
Ask	questions to learn more about a place: 1. Where is this place? 2. What is it like? 3. How have people changed the environment by their interaction with it? 4. How has the place been affected by the movement of people, goods, and ideas? 5. How is this place similar to and different from other places?	5 or more

Government

Skills/Strategies	Activity Suggestion	Foldable Parts
K-W-L	write about what you know, want to know, and learned about government	3
Define	government	1
Make a Venn diagram	of democracy (government where people make the laws and run the country), republic (a country where the people elect representatives to run the country), both, (or a democratic republic, such as the United States)	3
Find similarities	between a democratic republic and another form of government, such as communism	2
Make a time line	of the United States Constitution	any number
Explain	how the government gets its power from "the consent of the governed"	1
	how the governed give their consent	1
Show cause and effect	of voting in a democratic republic	2
List	responsibilities of our government: protect lives, protect property, enforce laws, provide schools, provide highways, etc.	any number
Describe	the three branches of government: executive, legislative, judicial	3
Differentiate between	the three levels of government: federal, state, and local	3
Give	examples of how levels of government work together for the good of the people	any number
Locate	Washington, D.C., on a map and a globe	1
	the capital of your state on a map of the U.S.	1
	your local government building on a city map	1

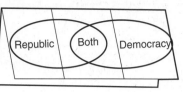

Three-tab Venn diagram

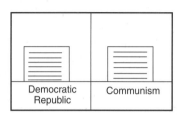

Pocket book

Pyramid fold

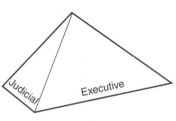

Trifold

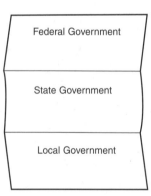

4x4 folded table

History

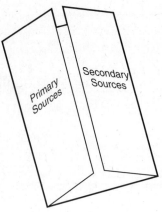

Shutter fold

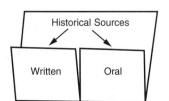

Concept map

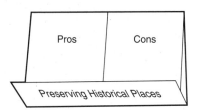

Two-tab matchbook

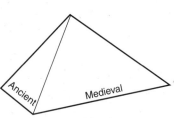

Pyramid fold

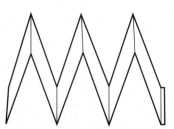

Time line:
"The History of Our Town"

Skills/Strategies	Activity Suggestion	Foldable Parts
K-W-L	write about what you know, want to know, and learned about history	3
Define	history	1
	historian	1
List	ways in which we can learn about the history of a location or country	any number
Differentiate between	primary and secondary sources	2
	written and oral sources	2
Compare	oral history, past and present	2
Explain	what is meant by distant past and recent past	2
Compare and contrast	different historical perspectives of an event	2
	past and recent history of a place	2
Justify	studying history	1
Notice	ways in which history is preserved in your family, community, state, and nation	any number
Describe	how time lines can be used to outline the history of a person, place, event, country, philosophy, government, etc.	any number
Report on	two historic markers in your community	2
List pros and cons	of preserving historic places	2
Investigate	artifacts and their importance to historians	any number
Research	the history of archaeology and explain how it helps us understand the past	2
	methods, tools, and technology used by archaeologists to help them understand artifacts and excavations	3
Find similarities and differences	between archaeologists and historians	2
	among archaeologists, historians, and paleontologists	3
Debate	how history can change	1

Holidays

Skills/Strategies	Activity Suggestion	Foldable Parts
K-W-L	write about what you know, want to know, and learned about holidays	3
Define	holiday	1
Research	the origins of three holidays, such as Arbor Day, Flag Day, and Kwanzaa	3

Classify	holidays that are the following:
	  religious observations
	  political or patriotic observations
	  commemorative or memorial of a person or a
	  group of people
		any number

Search	for holidays on a calendar	1
Mark	local or family holidays on your calendar	any number

Find	legal federal holidays on your calendar:
	  New Year's Day, January 1
	  Martin Luther King, Jr.'s, Birthday, January 15,
	    but observed on the third Monday in January
	  Washington's Birthday, February 22, but observed
	    on the third Monday in February
	  Memorial Day, the last Monday in May
	  Independence Day, July 4
	  Labor Day, the first Monday in September
	  Columbus Day, the second Monday in October
	  Veterans Day, November 11
	  Thanksgiving Day, the fourth Thursday in
	    November
	  Christmas Day, December 25
		10

Explain	why banks and schools also close on legal holidays	1
Determine	what happens when a legal holiday falls on a Sunday (the following Monday is usually observed as the holiday)	1

List	three examples of traditional holidays that are celebrated without the closing of federal offices, banks, and schools:
	  Valentine's Day, February 14
	  St. Patrick's Day, March 17
	  Halloween, October 31
		3

Make a Venn diagram	of legal holidays, traditional holidays, both	3
Compare and contrast	ways in which different cultures celebrate the same holiday	2
Make a time line	of the history of your favorite holiday	any number

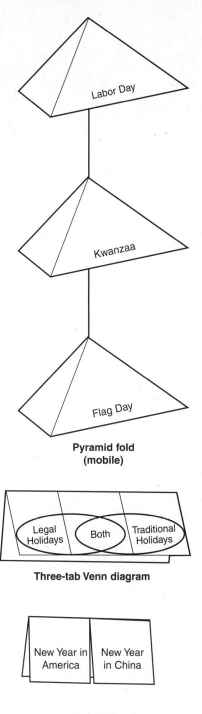

Pyramid fold (mobile)

Three-tab Venn diagram

Two-tab book

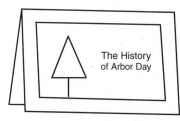

Picture frame book

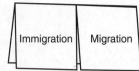

Immigration   Migration

Two-tab book

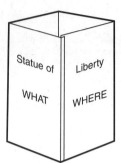

Statue of   Liberty

WHAT   WHERE

Standing cube

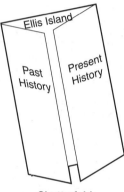

Ellis Island

Past History   Present History

Shutterfold

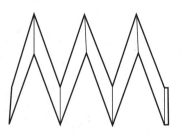

Time line:
"The History of Immigration"

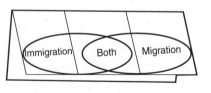

Immigration   Both   Migration

Three-tab Venn diagram

Immigration and Migration

Skills/Strategies	Activity Suggestion	Foldable Parts
K-W-L	write about what you know, want to know, and learned about immigration and migration	3
Define	immigration and migration	2
Make a Venn diagram	of immigration, migration, and both	3
Describe	how and why the first Americans might have migrated to North America	2
Research	the history of the Statue of Liberty	1
Locate	Ellis Island on a United States map (New York Harbor)	1
	Asian and Latin American countries on a map or globe and explain why large numbers of immigrants come to the United States from these countries	2
Compare and contrast	Ellis Island, past and present	2
Make a time line	of the history of migration and immigration to what is now the United States	any number
Graph	the numbers of immigrants entering the United States over a given period of time	any number
Investigate	the current population of the United States	1
Explain	how the motto of the United States, E pluribus unum ("Out of many, one"), relates to immigration	1

Important Documents

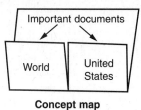

Concept map

Skills/Strategies	Activity Suggestion	Foldable Parts
K-W-L	write about what you know, want to know, and learned about important documents	3
Research	the "what, where, when, why/how" of:	
	Magna Carta, 1215	4
	Mayflower Compact, 1620	4
	Fundamental Orders of Connecticut, 1639	4
	Maryland Toleration Act, 1649	4
	Pennsylvania Frame of Government, 1682	4
	"Common Sense," Thomas Paine, 1774	4
	Declaration of Independence, July 4, 1776	4
	Articles of Confederation, 1781	4
	Constitution of the United States, 1789	4
	Bill of Rights, 1791	4
Make a time line	of important documents	any number
Compare and contrast	the importance of a document when it was written to its current importance	2
Investigate	documents important to the world	any number

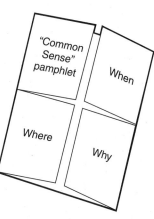

Four-door book

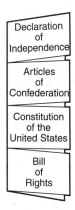

Four-tab book

Hot dog fold

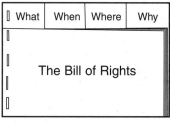

Top-tab book

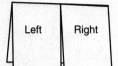

Two-tab book

Location

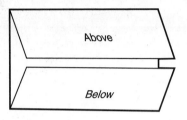

Shutter fold

Skills/Strategies	Activity Suggestion	Foldable Parts
K-W-L	write about what you know, want to know, and learned about location	3
Distinguish between	left and right and use these terms to tell directions	2

Use	position words to identify the location of things:
	    above, below
	    over, under
	    inside, outside
	    in front of, behind
	    on top, in the middle, at the bottom
		any number

Draw	a map to show the location of two or more things	2 or more
	a map to show a room in a building	2
Describe	the location of something using position words	any number
Note	that some things are always in the same location and some things move, or are mobile	2

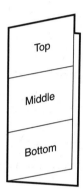

Three-tab book (vertical)

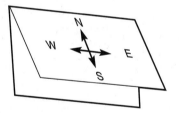

Half-book

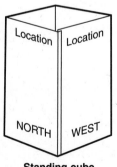

Standing cube

Map and Globe Skills

Skills/Strategies	Activity Suggestion	Foldable Parts
K-W-L	write about what you know, want to know, and learned about map and globe skills	3
Recognize	that a map is a drawing of a place	1
	that a model is a representation of something	1
Explain	the purpose of a map	1
List	three or more kinds of maps: city, world, road, treasure, etc.	3
Draw	a map of a room a map of a building	1
	a map to show how to get from one location to another	1
Use	a map to find the location of something	1
Trace	at least two routes on a map	2
Identify	7 continents on a map or globe	7
Position	a map so that it is easy to read and explain why you positioned it as you did	2
Find	things that are located close together and things that are far away from each other on a map	2
Compare and contrast	an aerial view of a location to a map of the same area	2
Describe	three things that make Earth different from the other planets in the Solar System: only planet known to have human, plant, and animal life	3
Differentiate between	land and water on a map or on the globe	2
Read	map symbols	any number
Use and draw	map keys	2
List	five or more things that are drawn on a map: towns, cities, rivers, roads, mountains, lakes, bridges, railroads, boundaries, etc.	5 or more

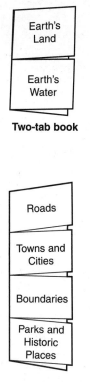

Two-tab book

Four-tab book

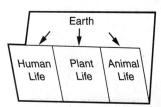

Concept map

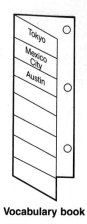

Vocabulary book

Me, Myself, I, and Others

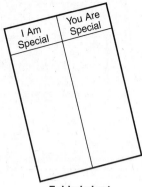

Folded chart

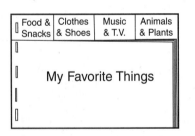

Pocket book

Bound book

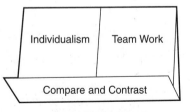

Top-tab book

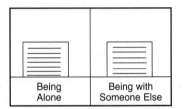

Two-tab matchbook

Skills/Strategies	Activity Suggestion	Foldable Parts
K-W-L	write about what you know, want to know, and learned about yourself	3
Define	characteristics and traits	2
chart	characteristics that make you special characteristics that make a friend special	2
Determine	why every living person is special	1
Explain	how you learn about yourself how you learn about others	2
List	things you are interested in and things you are not interested in	2
Describe	your favorite food, clothes, and entertainment	3
Compare and contrast	being alone and being with someone else	2
Find similarities and differences	between you and someone in your family	2
Classify	things you do when you work and things you do when you play	2
Make a time line	showing major events in your life	any number
Research	the "who, what, when, where" about yourself	4
Ask	someone to tell you stories about what you were like as a baby	any number
Make a Venn diagram	of you as a young child, you today, and both	3
Identify	things you can do alone and things that involve working with others	2

People

Skills/Strategies	Activity Suggestion	Foldable Parts
K-W-L	write about what you know, want to know, and learned about people	3
Describe	why people have jobs	1
List	different jobs people have	any number
Learn	the names of people you see regularly	any number
Explain	how all people can be alike and different	2
Compare and contrast	people, past and present	2
Recognize	that groups of people compose families, classes, school members, and organizations	4
Give examples	of racial, ethnic, and cultural groups	3

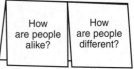

Two-tab book

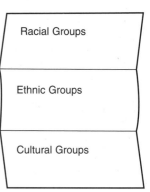

Trifold

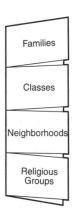

Four-tab book

4x4 Folded table

Places

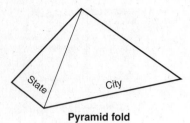

Pyramid fold

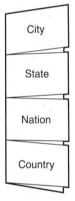

Places I've Been

Bound book

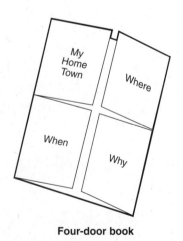

City

State

Nation

Country

Four-tab book

My Home Town   Where

When   Why

Four-door book

Skills/Strategies	Activity Suggestion	Foldable Parts
K-W-L	write about what you know, want to know, and learned about places	3
Explore	your school environment	1
	your home environment	1
	other safe environments	any number
Describe	three places you like to go	3
	the two parts of an address: street name and building number	2
Explain	three or more different types of homes: apartments, duplexes, trailer homes, single family homes, etc.	3 or more
Make a Venn diagram	of a home within a neighborhood	3
	of home, neighborhood, city	3
	of home, neighborhood, city, state	4
	of home, neighborhood, city, state, nation	5
	of home, neighborhood, city, state, nation, continent	6
	of neighborhood, city, state, nation, continent, world	6
Investigate	how places are named	any number
	how places are located	any number
Explain	home, address, street, neighborhood	4
Locate	five or more given places on a map or globe	5 or more

Natural Resources

Skills/Strategies	Activity Suggestion	Foldable Parts
K-W-L	write about what you know, want to know, and learned about natural resources	3
Define	natural resources	1
List	examples of natural resources	any number
	examples of renewable and nonrenewable natural resources	2
Explain	why the United States is said to be "rich in natural resources"	1
Describe	minerals, forests, wildlife, water, soil, sunlight, air, and fossil fuels as natural resources	6
Identify	natural resources found in each of the six regions of the United States: West, Mountain States, Southwest, Middle West, Southeast, Northeast	6
Compare and contrast	the natural resources of the United States to the natural resources of another country, such as Japan	2
Make a table	of the major natural resources of the seven continents: minerals, land, water, plants, wildlife, and fossil fuels	7
Investigate	ways in which natural resources are used for: food, fuel, and raw materials that are used for clothing and housing	3
Show cause and effect	of natural resources on imports and exports	2
Debate	whether the wealth of an area or nation is dependent upon its amount of natural resources	1
Research	the "who, what, when, where" of:	
	Theodore Roosevelt	4
	John Muir	4
Research	the "what, when, where, why" of:	
	the National Park System	4
	natural wildlife refuges	4
List pros and cons	of managing forest fires	2

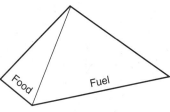

Two-tab book

Top-tab book

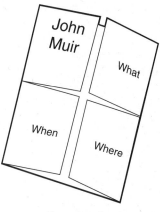

Pyramid fold

Four-door book

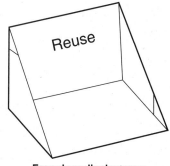

Four-door display case

Rules and Laws

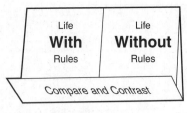

Two-tab matchbook

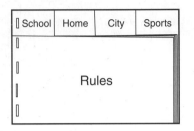

Top-tab book

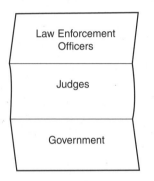

Trifold

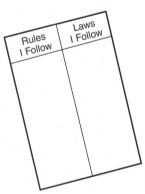

Folded chart

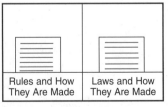

Pocket book

Skills/Strategies	Activity Suggestion	Foldable Parts
K-W-L	write about what you know, want to know, and learned about rules and laws	3
Explain	the importance of having rules	1
Chart	things that have rules and list examples of their rules: school, driving, playing games, etc.	any number
Compare and contrast	life with rules and life without rules	2
List	rules for your family/home and rules for your school	2
Describe	consequences of not following rules at home and at school	2
	how rules and laws keep people and property safe	2
Identify	three authority figures and explain their jobs	3
Discuss	laws as rules that outline a person's rights and obligations	2
Investigate	how laws: 1. outline a person's rights and obligations 2. set penalties for those who violate the laws 3. establish how government will enforce the laws and penalties	3
Explain	how laws might be changed and why they would need to be changed	2
Research	four or more governing groups that enforce laws: police departments, sheriffs and deputies, constables, and courts	4 or more
Differentiate between	what you would consider just and unjust laws	2
Compare and contrast	the laws of two different countries and explain why it is important to know the laws of other countries when traveling within their borders	2

Symbols

Skills/Strategies	Activity Suggestion	Foldable Parts
K-W-L	write about what you know, want to know, and learned about symbols	3
Describe	how symbols communicate ideas	1
Observe	five symbols in the world around you: letters of an alphabet, human gestures, flags, pictures and logos, etc.	5
List	examples of visual and auditory symbols	2
Research	symbols used in science and math	2
	symbols used by countries and governments	2
	symbols used by clubs or organizations	2
	symbols used by religions	any number
	symbols used by political parties	any number
	symbols used on highways	any number
Explain	how symbols develop meaning, positive and negative	2
Investigate	the development and use of international symbols	2
Make a table	of common state symbols: flower, bird, tree, flag, song, others	any number
Make a chart	of symbols that represent three countries	3
Draw	pictures of three symbols that represent the United States of America	3
Search	the Internet to learn the history of the swastika as a symbol, and outline its change from positive to negative symbolism	2
Investigate	five state symbols for at least five states: flag, flower, tree, motto, pledge, seal, bird, song, gem, stone, fossil, animals, etc.	5

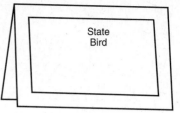

Picture frame book

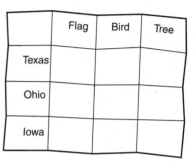

Folded table

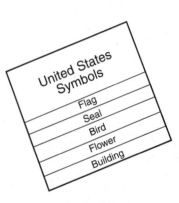

**Layered book
(3 sheets of paper)**

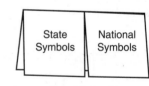

Two-tab book

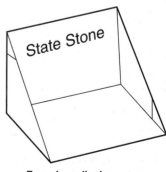

Four-door display case

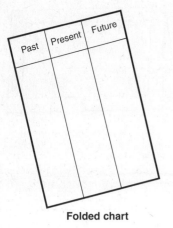

Folded chart

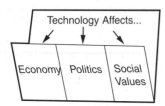

Concept map

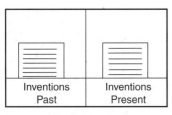

Pocket book

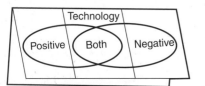

Three-tab Venn diagram

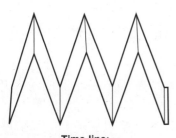

**Time line:
"History of Technology"**

Technology

Skills/Strategies	Activity Suggestion	Foldable Parts
K-W-L	write about what you know, want to know, and learned about technology	3
Define	technology	1
Explain	how technology helps people meet their needs and wants	2
	how technology has given people more time to pursue arts, science, sports, and hobbies	4
Discuss	how technology makes survival easier, but can also threaten survival	2
	how wealth affects access to and development of technology on a local and world level	2
Describe	how technology has influenced the history of the world	1
Make a Venn diagram	of primitive technology, advanced technology, and both	3
Outline	the technology of tool making	any number
Speculate	as to how technological advances spread, past and present. Examples include: trade, migration, writing, computers, etc.	any number
Research	the Stone Age, the Bronze Age, the Industrial Revolution, etc.	any number
List	three examples of problems that have resulted due to technological advances	3
Determine	how technology can affect a country's economic, political, and social values	3
Make a Venn diagram	of positive aspects of technology, negative aspects of technology, and both	3
Investigate	biotechnology	1
Find similarities and differences	between the history of inventions and the history of technology	2
Make a time line	on the history of technology	any number

Time

Skills/Strategies	Activity Suggestion	Foldable Parts
K-W-L	write about what you know, want to know, and learned about time	3
Use	terms to describe time:	
	past and present	2
	distant past, recent past, present	3
	past, present, future	3
Understand	seconds, minutes, hours, days	4
Use	days, weeks, months, and years to measure time	4
	years, decades, centuries, millenniums	4
Measure	the passing of time using a calendar	1
Explain	how one might make predictions about the future based upon the past	1
Note	how many times you need to know what time it is during a given amount of time	any number
Keep a journal	on how you spend your time	1
Research	the development of standardized time	1
	the history of the seven-day week	1
Classify	time zones and the International Date Line	2
Investigate	different tools used to measure time, past and present	2
Compare and contrast	a sundial and a water clock	2
Make a Venn diagram	of lunar time, solar time, and both	3
Make a time line	of the history of units used to measure time	any number

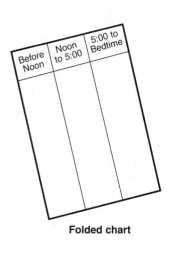

Folded table

Millenniums
Centuries
Decades
Years
Months
Weeks
Days
Hours
Minutes
Seconds

Layered book (5 sheets of paper)

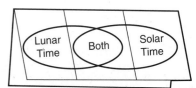

Three-tab Venn diagram

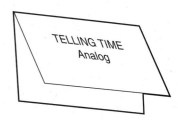

Folded chart

TELLING TIME Analog

Half-book

Transportation

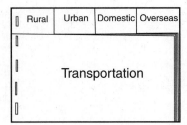

Top-tab book

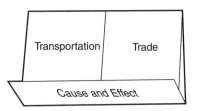

Two-tab Matchbook

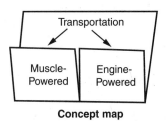

Concept map

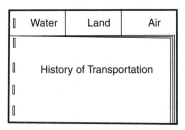

Top-tab Book

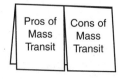

Two-tab book

Skills/Strategies	Activity Suggestion	Foldable Parts
K-W-L	write about what you know, want to know, and learned about transportation	3
Define	transportation	1
Explain	how and why transportation moves people	2
	how and why transportation moves goods that people need or want	2
Show cause and effect	between transportation and trade	2
	of transportation costs and cost of products and goods	2
	transportation and the development of towns and cities	2
Compare and contrast	methods of transportation involving people or animals and methods of transportation involving engines	2
Discuss	how the speed of transportation has changed over time	1
Investigate	methods of transportation powered by natural forces, such as wind and water	any number
Classify	the three main kinds of transportation: land, water, and air	3
Research	how the invention of the wheel changed transportation and civilization	1
	how the domestication of animals changed transportation and civilization	1
List pros and cons	of private transportation and public transportation	2
Explain	methods of urban, domestic, and overseas transportation	3
Determine	how transportation affects domestic freight and international freight	2
Make a time line	of the history of transportation	any number
Research	the "who, what, when, where" of:	
	Rudolf Diesel	4
	Orville Wright and Wilbur Wright	4
	Henry Ford	4

United States History

The following Social Studies topics are covered in this section:

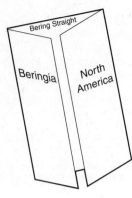

Shutter fold

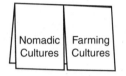

Two-tab book

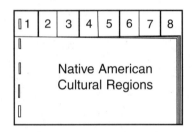

Top-tab book

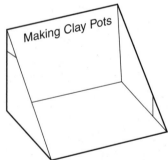

Four-door display case

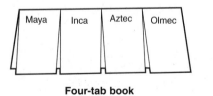

Four-tab book

First Americans

Skills/Strategies	Activity Suggestion	Foldable Parts
K-W-L	write about what you know, want to know, and learned about the first Americans	3
Describe	how the First Americans might have reached the North American continent and why they came	2
Locate	Beringia and the Bering Strait on a map or globe	2
Compare and contrast	nomadic cultures and farming cultures	2
	temporary villages and permanent villages	2
Research	the "what, where, why, when" of:	
	the Maya	4
	the Aztec	4
	the Mound Builders	4
	the Anasazi	4
	the Inca	4
Compare and contrast	the Mound Builders of the Southeast and the Anasazi of the Southwest	2
Research	the Native American cultural regions of the United States: 1. Arctic 2. Subarctic 3. Northwest Coast 4. California 5. Basin and Plateau 6. Southwest 7. Plains 8. Eastern Woodlands	8
Make a time line	of Maya history	any number
	of the Inca history	any number
	of the Aztec history	any number

Native Americans

Skills/Strategies	Activity Suggestion	Foldable Parts
K-W-L	write about what you know, want to know, and learned about the Native Americans	3
Give examples	of ways in which Native Americans used their environment to meet their needs and wants	2
Research	past and present Native American tribes of the following regions: West, Southwest, Plains, and Woodlands	4
	the government and laws of a group of Native American peoples, such as the Iroquois	2
Locate	the Northwest Coast of the United States on a map and speculate how Native Americans in this region met their needs	2
Read to discover	three technological developments of Native Americans: dams, canoes, bridges, traps, harvesting aids, irrigation, etc.	3
	three forms of transportation used by Native People	3
	two or more forms of communication used	2
	two or more types of currency used	2
	three or more kinds of structures built	3
Make a time line	of the history of a Native American people	any number
Make a Venn diagram	of Hopi, Tlinqit, of both	3
Describe	peaceful and warring Native American cultures	2
Outline	two early Native American encounters with Europeans	2
Compare and contrast	Native American life before and after reservations were established	2
Differentiate between	the roles of men and women among different Native American peoples	2
Show cause and effect	of a decline in Native American peoples across North America	2

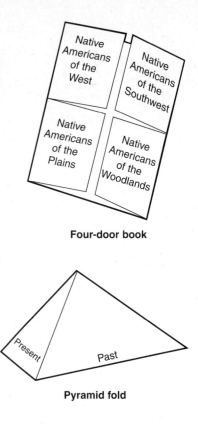

Four-door book

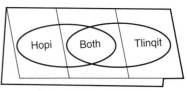

Pyramid fold

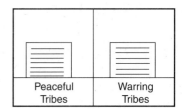

Three-tab Venn diagram

Pocket book

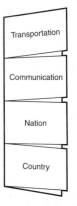

Four-tab book

Exploring the Americas

Half-book

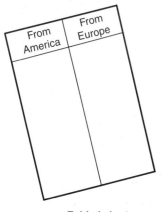

Folded chart

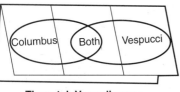

Three-tab Venn diagram

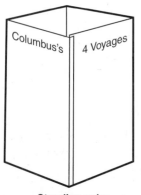

Standing cube

Skills/Strategies	Activity Suggestion	Foldable Parts
K-W-L	write about what you know, want to know, and learned about exploring the Americas	3
Describe	the Vikings and what they discovered as the first Europeans to explore the Western Hemisphere	2
Explain	how and why Columbus prepared for his first voyage	2
Investigate	the land and people first seen by Christopher Columbus (Taino people greeted Columbus on the island of San Salvador, also called Watling Island)	2
Debate	the statement "Columbus discovered America"	1
List	three effects of the "discovery" of the Western Hemisphere on the Native Americans and the explorers	3
Outline	the chain of events that took place after Columbus met the native people of North America	any number
Analyze	the effects of the exchange of cultures between Eastern and Western Hemispheres	2
Investigate	the Columbian Exchange:	
	listing plants and animals native to the Americas taken to Europe and then on to other countries by explorers: pineapple, tomatoes, corn, chili peppers, avocados, potatoes, pumpkins, turkeys, etc.	2
	listing plants and animals native to Europe brought to the Americas by explorers: wheat, peaches, cucumbers, oranges, grapes, sugar, horses, cattle, sheep, etc.	2
Make a Venn diagram	of Native Americans, first Europeans, and both	3
	of Columbus, Amerigo Vespucci, and both	3
Compare and contrast	Columbus's four voyages to the Western Hemisphere between 1492 and 1502	4
Research	the "who, what, when, where" of:	
	Christopher Columbus	4
	Amerigo Vespucci	4
	John Cabot	4
	Vicente Yanez Pinzon	4
	Pedro Alvares Cabral	4
	Vasco Núñez de Balboa	4

Conquering the Americas

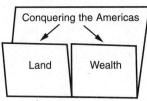
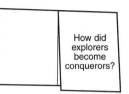

Concept map

Skills/Strategies	Activity Suggestion	Foldable Parts
K-W-L	write about what you know, want to know, and learned about the conquering of the Americas	3
Summarize	two motives for conquering the native peoples of the Americas, land and wealth	2
Map	the route Cortés took as he sailed across the Gulf of Mexico and into Mexico to Tenochtitlán	1
Outline	the events that led to the fall of Tenochtitlán	any number
Explain	how explorers became conquerors and differentiate between the two	2
Compare and contrast	Mexico before and after Hernando Cortés conquered the Aztec	2
	the conquerors and the conquered	2
Make a Venn diagram	Moctezuma, Hernando Cortéz, and both	3
Describe	Doña Marina and explain how she helped Hernando Cortés	2
Find similarities and differences	between Spain and New Spain	2
Research	the "who, what, when, where" of Bartolemé de las Casas, a Catholic priest and defender of Native American rights	4
Argue	against the encomienda system	1
Show cause and effect	of disease brought by the conquerors	2
Describe	how the search for gold expanded the lands of New Spain	1
Make a time line	to show the exploration and conquering of South America by Spanish and Portuguese conquistadors	any number
Research	the Inca civilization before and after Pizarro defeated Atahualpa and conquered the Incas	2

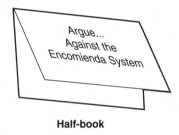

Three-quarter book

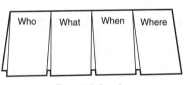

Half-book

Four-tab book

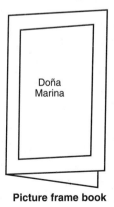

Picture frame book

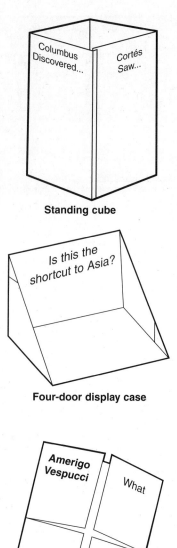

Standing cube

Columbus
Discovered...

Cortés
Saw...

Is this the
shortcut to Asia?

Four-door display case

Amerigo
Vespucci

What

When

Where

Four-door book

Explorers and Geography

Skills/Strategies	Activity Suggestion	Foldable Parts
Investigate	and describe how five explorers contributed to expanding the world's knowledge of the geography of Earth's surface (see next entry for a list of explorers)	5
Research	the "who, what, when, and where" of by the following explorers:	
	Hernando Cortés	4
	Juan Ponce de Leon	4
	Hernando de Soto	4
	Francisco Vasquez de Coronado	4
	Sebastian Cabot	4
	Francisco Pizarro	4
	Diego de Almagro	4
	Francisco de Orellana	4
	Amerigo Vespucci	4
	John Cabot	4
	Vicente Yanez Pinzón	4
	Pedro Alvares Cabral	4
	Vasco Núñez de Balboa	4
Investigate	two ways in which explorers reported their discoveries to others	2
Describe	an explorer's actions and the world's reactions to discoveries made	2
Make a table	of information on explorers, geographic discoveries made, and the outcome of the discoveries	3
Discover	when your community was first explored by Europeans and draw what you think they might have seen	2
Explain	how people native to the Americas could have been explorers within the Americas	1
Compare and contrast	Native American explorers and European explorers in the Americas	2
	mapmaking, past and present	2
Read and report	on the history of mapmaking	any number
Speculate	as to what is left for explorers and geographers to discover, report, and map	1

De
las
Casas

Picture frame book

Settlements in America

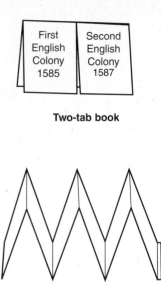

Two-tab book

Skills/Strategies	Activity Suggestion	Foldable Parts
K-W-L	write about what you know, want to know, and learned about the first settlements in America	3
Compare and contrast	England's first (1585) and second (1587) attempts to start colonies in America	2
Explain	why the search for a northwest passage was important, who attempted to discover it, and when it was finally accomplished (1906)	3
Determine	how the search for a northwest passage led to increased colonization of North America	1
Describe	how and why English, Dutch, and French colonists came to America	3
Show cause and effect	of the war between Spain and England and the colonization of America	2
Research	the Powhatan people, Chief Powhatan, and his daughter Pocahontas	3
Outline	the major events in the establishment of: Jamestown Colony, 1607	any number
	Plymouth Colony, 1620	any number
	Williamsburg, 1633	any number
Investigate	the celebration of thanksgiving held by the Pilgrims and the Wampanoag people in 1621 and compare it to celebrations held today	2
Locate	on a map the following areas of settlement: Roanoke Island; Jamestown, Virginia; St. Lawrence River; Hudson River; Plymouth, Massachusetts; Williamsburg, Virginia	6
Research	the "who, what, when, where" of:	
	John White	4
	Samuel de Champlain	4
	Henry Hudson	4
	the Pilgrims	4
	John Smith	4
	John Rolfe	4
Research	the "what, when, where, how" of the "Lost Colony" of Roanoke Island, 1587	4

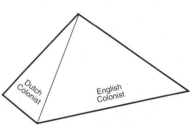

Time line: "Settlements in America"

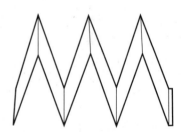

Pyramid fold

Time line: "Search for the Northwest Passage"

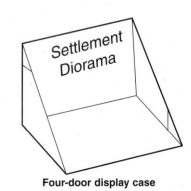

Four-door display case

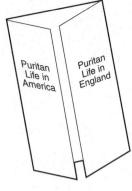

Shutter fold

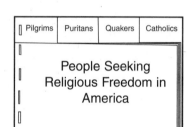

Top-tab book

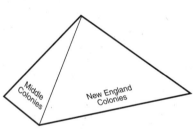

Pyramid

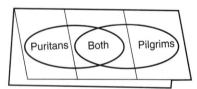

Three-tab Venn diagram

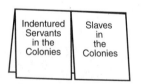

Two-tab book

Thirteen English Colonies

Skills/Strategies	Activity Suggestion	Foldable Parts
K-W-L	write about what you know, want to know, and learned about the thirteen colonies	3
Locate	the New England Colonies on a map: Connecticut, Massachusetts, New Hampshire, Rhode Island	4
Explain	three reasons why the Puritans wanted to leave England and come to America	3
Make a Venn diagram	of Puritans, Pilgrims, and both	3
Outline	the history of the New England Colonies, the Middle Colonies, and the Southern Colonies	3
Make a time line	that shows the establishment, development, and growth of all thirteen colonies	any number
Describe	how William Penn, a Quaker, started Philadelphia, which means "brotherly love"	1
	how the Dutch colony of New Netherland became the English colony of New York	1
Find	the four Middle Colonies on a map: New Jersey, New York, Pennsylvania, Delaware	4
Compare and contrast	the New England Colonies and Middle Colonies	2
	the Middle Colonies and Southern Colonies	2
	the New England Colonies and Southern Colonies	2
Sequence	the events that led to the founding of Georgia	any number
Determine	how groups of people seeking religious freedom influenced the development of the thirteen colonies: Pilgrims, Puritans, Quakers, and Catholics	4
Locate	the Southern Colonies on a map: Maryland, Virginia, North Carolina, South Carolina, Georgia	5
Find similarities and differences	between the relationships of colonists and Native Americans in the New England, Middle, and Southern Colonies	3
	between the economies of the colonies	2
Make a table	of information on the thirteen colonies: founder, reason for founding, location, natural resources, historic events	any number
Outline	the history of slavery in the English colonies	any number
Make a Venn diagram	of indentured servants, slaves, and both	3
Research	the "who, what, when, where" of:	
	John Winthrop	4
	Anne Hutchinson	4
	William Penn	4
	James Oglethorpe	4
	Lord Baltimore	4
	Metacomet, Wampanoag leader	4

Spain and France in North America

Skills/Strategies	Activity Suggestion	Foldable Parts
K-W-L	write about what you know, want to know, and learned about Spain and France in North America	3
Locate	on a map the territory claimed by France in the late 1600s	1
	the territory claimed by Spain in the late 1600s	1
Make a time line	of the history of St. Augustine, Florida (Spain's first settlement in current United States)	any number
Define	mission	1
List and desscribe	two purposes of Spanish missions: to convert Native Americans to the Catholic religion and to demonstrate Spain's ownership of land	2
Research	three of the Spanish missions built in North America between the late 1500s and early 1800s	3
Locate	El Camino Real, or the road between New Mexico and Mexico, on a map and note the missions built along the route	2
Compare and contrast	Spanish California and Spanish Texas	2
Explain	how the fur trade brought wealth and power to France	2
Compare and contrast	the French and Spanish relations with Native Americans	2
Make a time line	and research at least four French colonies and trading posts that became North American cities: Quebec St. Louis Detroit Chicago	4
Investigate	how French settlements, forts, and trading posts prohibited the expansion of English colonies	3
Compare and contrast	the French colonies and English colonies in North America	2
	the English colonies and Spanish colonies in North America	2
	the Spanish colonies and English colonies in North America	2
Make a Venn diagram	of New Spain, New France, and both	3
Research	the "who, what, when, where" of:	
	Robert La Salle	4
	Samuel de Champlain	4
	Jacques Marquette	4
	Louis Jolliet	4
	Jean Baptiste Point du Sable	4

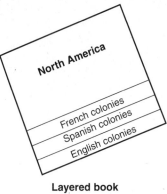

Layered book (2 sheets of paper)

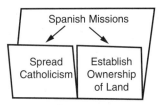

Concept map

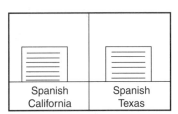

Pocket book

Picture frame book

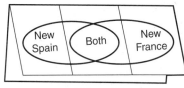

Three-tab Venn diagram

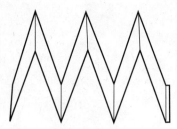

Time line:
"The French and Indian War"

France After the War

England After the War

Spain After the War

Three-tab book
(vertical)

The French and Indian War

Skills/Strategies	Activity Suggestion	Foldable Parts
K-W-L	write about what you know, want to know, and learned about The French and Indian War	3
Explain	how the French and Indian War got its name, when it started, and why	3
Describe	who led the Virginia colonists in the French and Indian War—George Washington	1
Outline	the major events of the French and Indian War 1754–1763	any number
Compare and contrast	Indian relations with the French and the British	2
Mark	the boundaries of the British colonies before and after the French and Indian War	2
List	three resources that helped the British win the war	3
Summarize	the terms of the Treaty of Paris (1763)	1
Discuss	the positions of France, England, and Spain at the end of the French and Indian War	3
Research	Pontiac's Rebellion (1763)	1
Research	the "who, what, when, where" of:	
	George Washington	4
	General Edward Braddock	4
	Pontiac	4

George Washington

What

When

Where

Four-door book

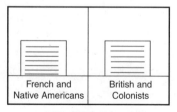

French and Native Americans

British and Colonists

Pocket book

American Revolution

Skills/Strategies	Activity Suggestion	Foldable Parts
K-W-L	write about what you know, want to know, and learned about the American Revolution	3
Compare and contrast	self-government of the colonies and the government of England	2
	the British Army and American (Continental) Army	2
Explain	why the colonies rebelled against Great Britain: 1. the British government refused to allow colonists to move west of the Appalachian Mountains 2. taxation without representation	2
Define	liberty and explain what it meant to the colonists	2
Describe	British actions and colonial reactions that contributed to the revolution	2
Research	the "who, what, when, where" of:	
	the Sons of Liberty	4
	the Boston Tea Party	4
	African American Soldiers in the Continental Army	4
Make a Venn diagram	of the Stamp Act, Townshend Acts, and both	3
	of the First Continental Congress, Second Continental Congress, and both	3
	of battles on land, battles at sea, and both	3
Outline	the major battles of the America Revolution	any number
Show cause and effect	of the first two battles of the American Revolution, Lexington and Concord	2
Investigate	three authors of the Declaration of Independence: Thomas Jefferson, John Adams, Benjamin Franklin, Roger Sherman, and Robert Livingston	5
Differentiate	between Patriots, Loyalists, Neutrals	3
List	strengths and weaknesses of the British and Continental Armies	4
Explain	why the French decided to support the colonists in 1778 and the Spanish in 1779	2
Investigate	the Battle of Yorktown (1781) and the conditions of the Treaty of Paris (1783)	2
Make a time line	of the American Revolution, 1775–1783	any number
Research	the "who, what, when, where" of:	
	Patrick Henry	4
	Samuel Adams	4
	Abigail Adams	4
	Henry Knox	4
	Paul Revere and William Dawes	4
	George Rogers Clark	4
	John Paul Jones	4

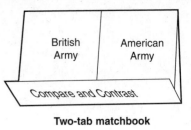

Two-tab matchbook

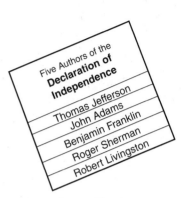

**Layered book
(3 sheets of paper)**

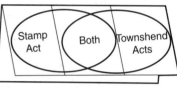

Three-tab Venn diagram

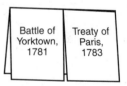

Two-tab book

Four-door book

The Constitution

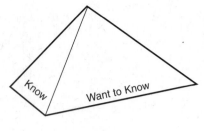

Pyramid fold

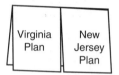

Two-tab book

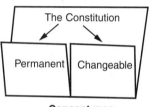

Concept map

Seven Articles of the Constitution
Article I
Article II
Article III
Article IV
Article V
Article VI
Article VII

**Layered book
(four sheets of paper)**

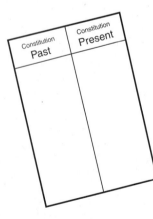

Folded chart

Skills/Strategies	Activity Suggestion	Foldable Parts
K-W-L	write about what you know, want to know, and learned about the Constitution	3
Explain	why Americans were afraid of strong central government after years of British rule	1
Describe	the strengths and weaknesses of the Articles of Confederation	2
Compare and contrast	the Virginia Plan and the New Jersey Plan	2
	the concerns of "large" and "small" states	2
Find similarities and differences	between the delegates to the Continental Convention	2
Make a Venn diagram	of the Articles of Confederation, the Constitution, and both	3
Summarize	the Great Compromise and other compromises made at the Constitution Convention	any number
Explain	how the Constitution is permanent and yet changeable	2
	the system of checks and balances	2
Describe	the importance of the Constitution, past and present	2
Summarize	the seven articles of the Constitution	7
Research	four or more of the 27 Amendments to the Constitution	4 or more
Sequence	the events that led to the development of the Constitution; its signing by the Constitutional delegates on September 17, 1787; its ratification; and its amendments	4
Research	the "who, what, when, where" of:	
	Alexander Hamilton	4
	James Madison	4
	George Mason	4
	Roger Sherman	4

A New Nation

Half-book

Skills/Strategies	Activity Suggestion	Foldable Parts
K-W-L	write about what you know, want to know, and learned about the new nation called United States of America	3
Outline	the history of the District of Columbia and the city of Washington, D.C.	2
Research	the Presidencies of George Washington, John Adams, Thomas Jefferson, James Madison, and James Monroe	5
List	two reasons for rapid population growth after independence	2
Argue	for and against the purchase of unknown land for $15 million dollars	2
Map	the exploration route of the Lewis and Clark the expedition, 1804–1806	1
Compare and contrast	the center of the country in 1800 and today	2
List	the states of the United States in 1801 (16)	16
Research	the "what, where, when, why/how" of the Louisiana Purchase (1803)	4
Research	the "who, what, where, when" of:	
	Meriwether Lewis	4
	William Clark	4

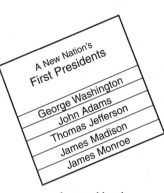

**Layered book
(3 sheets of paper)**

Standing cube

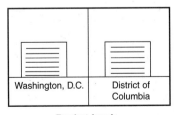

Pocket book

The War of 1812

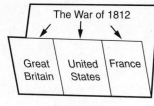

The War of 1812

Great Britain | United States | France

Concept map

British Navy — Both — U.S. Navy

Three-tab Venn diagram

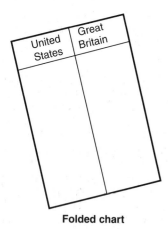

Victory at Fort McHenry | Victory at the Battle of New Orleans

Standing cube

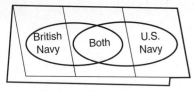

United States | Great Britain

Folded chart

Great Britain

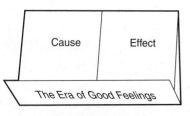

Cause | Effect

The Era of Good Feelings

Two-tab matchbook

Skills/Strategies	Activity Suggestion	Foldable Parts
K-W-L	write about what you know, want to know, and learned about the War of 1812	3
Show cause and effect	of the War of 1812	2
Describe	Great Britain, France, and United States involvement in the War of 1812	3
Differentiate between	War Hawks and Neutrals	2
Make a Venn diagram	of the British Navy, U.S. Navy, and both	3
Compare and contrast	the war on land and the war at sea	2
Sketch	the USS *Constitution*, also called "Old Ironsides," and explain how it was used during the war	2
Describe	what it would have been like to be in Washington, D.C., as the British advanced and burned the city	1
Research	the role of Native Americans in this war	1
Recite	"The Star Spangled Banner" and investigate its history	2
List	at least two reasons why the United States tried to invade Canada during this war	2
Outline	four United States victories: 1. Victory of the USS *Constitution* 2. Victory on Lake Erie 3. Victory at Fort McHenry 4. Victory at the Battle of New Orleans	4
Make a time line	of the major events of the War of 1812	any number
Explain	the cause and effect of the Era of Good Feelings that followed the end of the War of 1812	2
Summarize	what the United States gained from this war	1
Research	the "who, what, when, where" of Commodore Oliver Hazard Perry	4
	the "what, when, where, why/how" of the United States national anthem	4

Westward Expansion

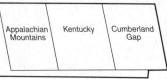

Three-tab book

Skills/Strategies	Activity Suggestion	Foldable Parts
K-W-L	write about what you know, want to know, and learned about westward expansion	3
Define	*pioneers* and explain their importance to American expansion	2
	frontier and explain how frontiers shifted over time	2
Show cause and effect	between the growing population of the United States and migration to lands west of the Appalachian Mountains from 1770–1790	2
Locate	on a map or globe: Appalachian Mountains, Kentucky, Cumberland Gap	3
List	reasons for westward expansion	any number
Investigate	the Era of Good Feelings and the Monroe Doctrine (1823)	2
Read about	Andrew Jackson before and after he became President	2
Classify	things that occurred during Jackson's Presidency as either positive or negative	2
Discuss	attitudes toward Native Americans during the first and last half of the 1800s	any number
Research	the Cherokee, Choctaw, Chickasaw, Muscogee, and Seminole communities in the early 1800s	5
Locate	Indian Territory on a map or globe	1
Illustrate	how the western boundary of the United States changed over time: Appalachian Mountains, Mississippi River, Rocky Mountains, Pacific Ocean	4
Explain	how Texas became part of the United States	1
Summarize	important events in Texas history that occurred on the following dates: 1821, 1836, 1845	3
Draw	a map showing the boundaries of the United States before and after the Mexican War	2
Argue	for and against the idea of "manifest destiny"	2
Make a time line	of the main events in the two-year war with Mexico	any number
Investigate	the Oregon Trail, the Mormon Trail, and the California Trail	3
Show the cause and effect	of the discovery of gold in California in 1849	2
Research	the "who, what, when, where" of:	
	Daniel Boone	4
	Abraham Lincoln	4
Research	the "what, where, when, how/why" of:	
	the Wilderness Road	4
	the Trail of Tears	4
	the Treaty of Guadalupe Hidalgo (1848)	4

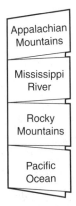

Standing cube

Four-tab book

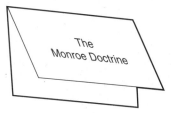

Half-book

Two-tab book

Industrial Revolution

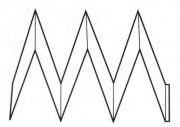

Time line:
"The Industrial Revolution"

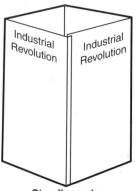

Three-tab Venn diagram

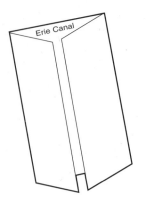

Standing cube

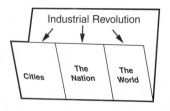

Shutter fold

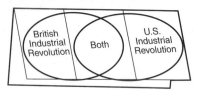

Concept map

Skills/Strategies	Activity Suggestion	Foldable Parts
K-W-L	write about what you know, want to know, and learned about the Industrial Revolution	3
Show cause and effect	of the Industrial Revolution	2
List	ways in which the Industrial Revolution changed how people lived and worked	2
Note	that the Industrial Revolution began in 1790, shortly after the American Revolution ended, and determine the importance of the timing	2
Determine	positive and negative effects of the Industrial Revolution	2
Make a time line	of the Industrial Revolution	any number
Make a Venn diagram	of the British Industrial Revolution, the U.S. Industrial Revolution, and both	3
Research	the "who, what, when, where" of:	
	Samuel Slater	4
	Eli Whitney	4
	Francis Cabot Lowell	4
	Cyrus McCormick	4
	John Deere	4
	Robert Fulton	4
Research	the advantages and disadvantages of a free market	2
	Massachusetts as the leading manufacturing state in the early 1800s and determine the leading manufacturing state today	2
Explain	how faster production lowers the cost of products	2
	the importance of interchangeable parts	1
Investigate	four inventions, such as the cotton gin, the reaper, the steam engine, the self-scouring plow	4
Investigate	how the Industrial Revolution changed transportation on land and on water	2
Outline	the history of the Erie Canal	any number
Show the cause and effect	of lower transportation costs and increased trade	2

Slavery

Skills/Strategies	Activity Suggestion	Foldable Parts
K-W-L	write about what you know, want to know, and learned about slavery in America	3
Compare and contrast	lifestyles in the northern and southern parts of the United States in the mid-1800s	2
	the lives of indentured servants and poor immigrants to the lives of slaves	2
	the needs of a manufacturing society to the needs of an agricultural society	2
Describe	opportunities for work in the North and the South	2
Explain	how the question of slavery deeply divided the United States in the 1850s	1
List	some of the arguments for and against slavery	2
Research	the "who, what, when, where" of:	
	Nat Turner	4
	Frederick Douglass	4
	William Lloyd Garrison	4
	Angelina Grimke and Sarah Grimke	4
	Harriet Tubman	4
	Levi Coffin and Catherine Coffin	4
	Sojourner Truth	4
	Harriet Beecher Stowe	4
	John Brown	4
Make a Venn diagram	of lives of free African Americans, lives of enslaved African Americans, and both	3
Compare and contrast	attitudes towards African Americans in the North and in the South before the Civil War	2
	attitudes after the Civil War	2
Investigate	past and present African American publications	2
Define and describe	the abolitionist movement	2
Research	the "what, when, where, why/how" of:	
	Freedom's Journal	4
	Underground Railroad	4
	The Liberator, an abolitionist newspaper	4
	Harper's Ferry	4
	Dred Scott decision	4
	Uncle Tom's Cabin	4
Make a Venn diagram	of the Abolitionist Movement, the Women's Rights Movement, and both	3
Chart	free states and slave states in the 1850s	2
Summarize	the Missouri Compromise of 1820, the Compromise of 1850, and the Kansas-Nebraska Act of 1854	3

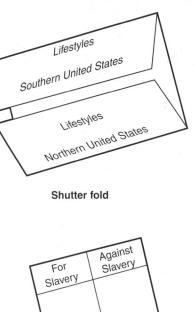

Shutter fold

Folded chart

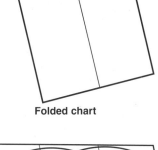

Three-tab Venn diagram

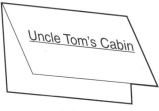

Half-book

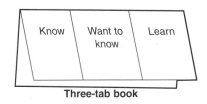

Three-tab book

The Civil War

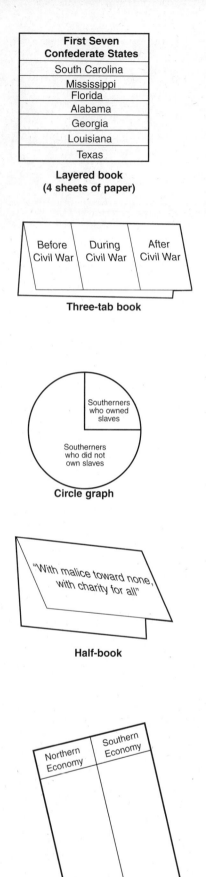

First Seven Confederate States

First Seven Confederate States
South Carolina
Mississippi
Florida
Alabama
Georgia
Louisiana
Texas

Layered book (4 sheets of paper)

Before Civil War | During Civil War | After Civil War

Three-tab book

Southerners who owned slaves

Southerners who did not own slaves

Circle graph

"With malice toward none, with charity for all"

Half-book

Northern Economy | Southern Economy

Folded chart

Skills/Strategies	Activity Suggestion	Foldable Parts
K-W-L	write about what you know, want to know, and learned about the Civil War	3
List	the seven states that seceded to form the Confederate States of America	7
Show cause and effect	of Abraham Lincoln's being elected President in 1860	2
	of differing opinions on states' rights and slavery	2
Research	the "who, what, when, where" of:	
	Abraham Lincoln	4
	Jefferson Davis	4
	Robert E. Lee	4
	Ulysses S. Grant	4
	Rose Greenhow, Confederate spy	4
	Blanche Bruce and Hiram Revels	4
	William Tecumseh Sherman	4
	Robert Gould Shaw	4
Research	the "what, where, when, why/how" of:	
	Fort Sumter	4
	Emancipation Proclamation	4
	Gettysburg Address	4
	Appomattox, Virginia	4
	Freedman's Bureau	4
Describe	events occurring before, during, and after the Civil War	3
	the armies of the North and the South	2
List	Northern and Southern victories	2
Make a time line	of the key events of the Civil War	any number
Compare	the strengths of the North and the South	2
Graph	the number of Southerners who owned slaves	1
Define	blockade and describe how it might be used in war	2
Outline	how technology changed the way wars were fought	any number
Investigate	the *Monitor* and the *Merrimack*	2
Describe	two of the battles of the Civil War: Antietam, Shiloh, Vicksburg, Gettysburg, etc.	2
	the 54th Massachusetts Colored Regiment	1
Locate	Appomattox, Virginia, on a map	1
Make a Venn diagram	Ulysses Grant, Robert E. Lee, and both	3
Write	about the meaning of "With malice toward none, with charity for all"	1
Summarize	the Thirteenth, Fourteenth, and Fifteenth Amendments	3
Describe	how Reconstruction affected blacks and whites in the South	2
List	events before, during, and after Reconstruction	3

The Western Frontier

Skills/Strategies	Activity Suggestion	Foldable Parts
K-W-L	write about what you know, want to know, and learned about America's western frontier	3
Define	homesteader	1
Locate	three areas where homesteaders established new towns during the 1860s	3
	three large cattle towns on a map or globe: Abilene, Texas; Fort Worth, Texas; Dodge City, Kansas	3
	the path of the transcontinental railroad	1
Describe	how the transcontinental railroad started on the east and west coasts and met at a point in the middle	1
Research	the "what, when, where, why/how" of:	
	Promontory Point, Utah	4
	Chisholm Trail	4
	Homestead Act of 1862	4
Make a time line	of the key events in the building of the first transcontinental railroad	any number
	of the history of cattle ranching	any number
Show cause and effect	of the transcontinental railroad and the economic growth of the west and the whole United States	2
Explain	how railroads made travel faster, cheaper, and safer in the 1800s	3
Research	the "who, what, when, where" of:	
	Grenville Dodge	4
	Charles Crocker	4
	Chief Joseph	4
	George Custer	4
List	two problems encountered while building the transcontinental railroad and their solutions	2
Discover	two ways the cattle industry changed the West	2
	two ways in which railroads affected the cattle industry	2
Outline	key events in the Plains Wars	any number
Make a Venn diagram	of Native Americans, the settlers, and both	3
Make a concept map	showing the decline of buffalo due to railroads, cattle drives, and new settlers	3
Sequence	Native Americans living on land, Native Americans being forced onto reservations by government, new settlers moving onto the land	3

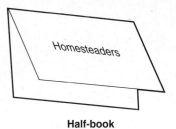

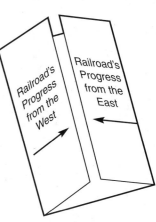

Half-book

Shutter fold

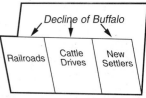

Concept map

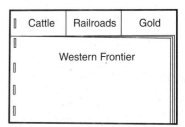

Top tab book

Two-tab book

Urbanization and Immigration

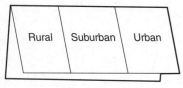

Three-tab book

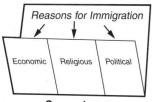

Pocket book

Reasons for Immigration

Economic | Religious | Political

Concept map

| Why | When | How | Where |

Interview with an Immigrant:

Felix Martinez

Top-tab book

Skills/Strategies	Activity Suggestion	Foldable Parts
K-W-L	write about what you know, want to know, and learned about America's rural, urban, and suburban areas	3
Make a Venn diagram	of rural, urban, and suburban	3
Compare and contrast	life in rural areas and urban areas in the 1700s	2
	life in rural and urban areas in the 1800s	2
	life in rural and urban areas in the 1900s	2
	life in rural and urban areas today	2
Predict	future trends in population distribution in your area	1
List	reasons cities grow and cities decline	2
Explain	why immigrants tend to move to cities	1
	why farming communities declined during the 1900s	1
Describe	the impact of immigration and immigrants on a city	2
	settlement houses, slums, and tenements	3
Research	Ellis Island and Angel Island and locate them on a map	2
Research	the "who, what, when, where" of: Jane Addams	4
Research	the "what, where, when, why/how" of:	
	the Great Chicago Fire	4
	Hull House, the first settlement house	4
Outline	two or more things immigrants had to do before they were allowed to enter the country	2 or more
Graph	the percentage of Americans living on a farm in 1800, 1900, and 2000	3
Investigate	three reasons why people immigrate from one place to another: economic, religious, political	3
Speculate	as to what was meant by the terms "old country" and "new country"	2
Interview	someone who has recently immigrated to the United States: Why did he or she come? When did he or she come? How did he or she come? Where did he or she come from? What does he or she think of America?	any number
Research	past and present efforts to limit immigration	2

Inventions and Technology

Skills/Strategies	Activity Suggestion	Foldable Parts
K-W-L	write about what you know, want to know, and learned about changes brought on by inventions and technology	3
Present	five examples of how inventions have changed the world since prehistoric times	5
Explain	how inventions can change lifestyles for better and for worse	2
Make a time line	outlining the major events in the history of inventions	any number
Research	the "who, what, when, where" of:	
	Benjamin Franklin	4
	Thomas Alva Edison	4
	Alexander Graham Bell	4
	Lewis Latimer	4
	Elijah McCoy	4
	Orville Wright and Wilbur Wright	4
	Henry Ford	4
Invent	something, describe your invention, and plan marketing and promotion	3
Research	inventions of the 1700s inventions of the 1800s inventions of the 1900s	3
Predict	how future inventions might change civilization	1
Outline	how inventions and technology changed land and air transportation	2

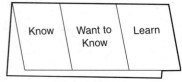

Three-tab book

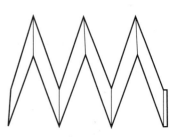

Time line: "Inventions and Technology"

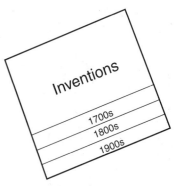

Layered book (2 sheets of paper)

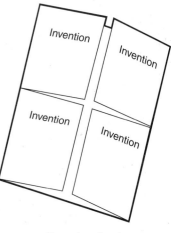

Four-door book

Business and Industry

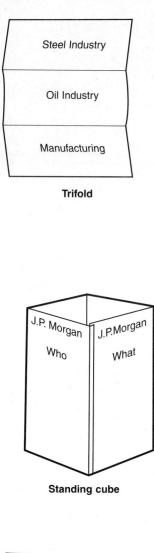

Trifold

Standing cube

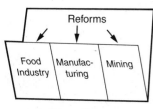

Two-tab book

Concept map

Skills/Strategies	Activity Suggestion	Foldable Parts
K-W-L	write about what you know, want to know, and learned about business and industry at the beginning of the 20th century	3
Research	the "who, what, when, where" of:	
	Andrew Carnegie	4
	John D. Rockefeller	4
	J. P. Morgan	4
	Mary Harris Jones	4
	Samuel Compers	4
Research	the "what, where, when, why" of:	
	American Federation of Labor, AFL	4
	Sherman Anti-Trust Act, 1890	4
	assembly lines	4
Show the cause and effect	of the technological advances and the growth of large companies	2
research	the history of the use of iron and steel	2
	the cause and effect of prosperity during the 1920s	2
Compare and contrast	the steel industry, the oil industry, and manufacturing	3
	the jobs and work in the 1700s and the 1800s	4
	past and present use of child labor in America and the world	4
Make a Venn diagram	of corporation, partnership, and both	3
Describe	corporation and shareholders	2
List	pros and cons of a monopoly	2
	reasons monopolies are built and broken	2
Outline	the history of the labor movement and unions	any number
	the reform movement to eliminate and control unfair business practices	any number
Show the cause and effect	of "muckrakers"	2
Investigate	important reforms in the food industry, manufacturing, and mining	3
Find similarities and differences	between factory jobs and farm work	2

Expansion

Skills/Strategies	Activity Suggestion	Foldable Parts
K-W-L	write about what you know, want to know, and learned about the expansion of the United States	3
Describe	the new territories gained by the United States in the late 1800s, Alaska and Hawaii	2
Compare and contrast	Alaska and Hawaii before and after they became states	2
Make a time line	of the history: of Alaska of Hawaii	any number
Identify	two causes of the Spanish-American War (1898)	2
Analyze	two consequences of the Spanish-American War	2
Investigate	what territories the United States gained in the Spanish-American War: Puerto Rico, Guam, and the Philippines	3
Research	the "what, when, where, why/how" of:	
	the USS *Maine*	4
	Rough Riders	4
Research	the "who, what, when, where" of":	
	James Cook	4
	Queen Liliuokalani	4
	William Seward	4
	William McKinley	4
	Theodore Roosevelt	4
	George Dewey	4
Locate on a map	the lands controlled by the United States by 1900: Alaska, Aleutian Islands, Hawaiian Islands, Johnston Island, Baker Island, American Samoa, Wake Island, Midway Islands, Guam, Philippine Islands, Puerto Rico	11
Make a time line	of the history of the Panama Canal	any number
List pros and cons	of the United States buying a 10-mile-wide strip of land called the Canal Zone	2
Investigate	why the United States bought the Virgin Islands from Denmark during World War I	1

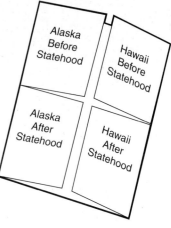

Four-door book

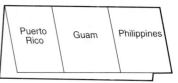

Three-tab book

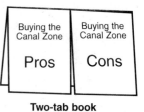

Two-tab book

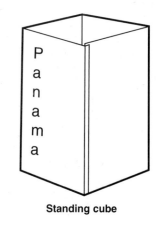

Standing cube

World War I

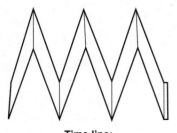

Time line:
"Key Events of World War I"

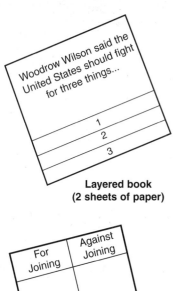

Woodrow Wilson said the
United States should fight
for three things...

1
2
3

Layered book
(2 sheets of paper)

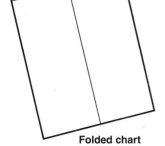

For
Joining

Against
Joining

Folded chart

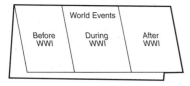

World Events

Before
WWI

During
WWI

After
WWI

Three-tab book

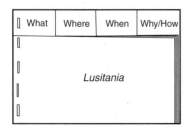

What | Where | When | Why/How

Lusitania

Top-tab book

Skills/Strategies	Activity Suggestion	Foldable Parts
K-W-L	write about what you know, want to know, and learned about World War I	3
Make a time line	of key events of World War I	any number
Find similarities and differences	between the Allied Powers and the Central Powers	2
Sequence	two key events that led the United States into WWI	2
Research	the "who, what, when, where" of: Woodrow Wilson	4
Research	the "what, where, when, why/how" of:	
	Lusitania	4
	the Treaty of Versailles (1919)	4
	the League of Nations	4
Outline	three things Woodrow Wilson said the United States should fight for: 1. democracy 2. rights and liberties of small nations 3. the right of free peoples to bring peace and safety to all nations	3
Describe	two ways in which World War I changed the United States	2
	world events before, during, and after WWI	3
Research	the design and use of German U-boats, war planes, and tanks	3
Debate	the use of poison gas	2
Locate	the following on a map or globe: Britain, France, Italy, Belgium and Russia (Allies) Germany, Austria-Hungary, Turkey (Central Powers) Virgin Islands Atlantic Ocean Versailles, France	any number
Make a Venn diagram	of weapons of the Civil War, World War I, and both	3
Compare and contrast	hardships on the war front and the home front	2
Outline	three ways in which the Treaty of Versailles affected Germany: 1. Took away Germany's colonies 2. Redrew Germany's nation borders 3. Required Germany to pay fines to the Allied Powers	3
Argue	for and against the United States joining the League of Nations after World War I	2
Investigate	Veterans Day and explain what it commemorates	2

Between World Wars

Skills/Strategies	Activity Suggestion	Foldable Parts
K-W-L	write about what you know, want to know, and learned about the years between World War I and World War II	3
Research	the "who, what, when, where" of:	
	Calvin Coolidge	4
	Franklin Delano Roosevelt	4
	Charles Lindbergh	4
	Duke Ellington	4
	F. Scott Fitzgerald	4
	Amelia Earhart	4
Investigate	the rapid growth of three types of media during this time: radio, newspapers, magazines	3
Show cause and effect	between growth in media and growth in the advertising industry	3
	between improved transportation and increase in travel	2
Describe	key events in the three terms of President Franklin Delano Roosevelt	3
Research	the first non-stop, solo flight across the Atlantic, completed by Charles Lindbergh in May 1917	1
Compare and contrast	methods of communication in the 1920s and today	2
	methods of transportation in the 1920s and today	2
	celebrities of the 1920s and today	2
Make a time line	of the history of the use of electricity	any number
Explain	two ways in which women's lives changed during this time	2

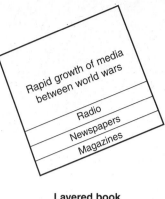

**Layered book
(2 sheets of paper)**

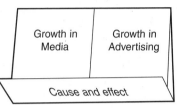

Two-tab matchbook

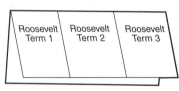

Three-tab book

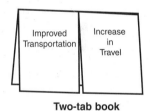

Two-tab book

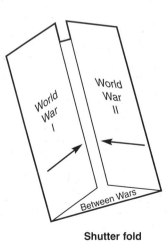

Shutter fold

The Great Depression

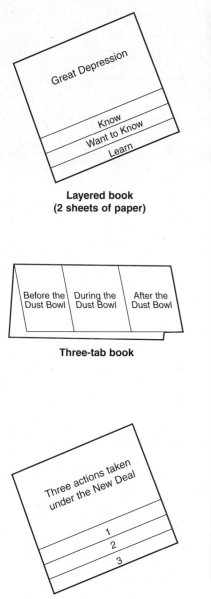

Great Depression

Know

Want to Know

Learn

**Layered book
(2 sheets of paper)**

Before the
Dust Bowl | During the
Dust Bowl | After the
Dust Bowl

Three-tab book

**Three actions taken
under the New Deal**

1

2

3

**Layered book
(2 sheets of paper)**

Skills/Strategies	Activity Suggestion	Foldable Parts
K-W-L	write about what you know, want to know, and learned about the Great Depression	3
Make a time line	of key events of Great Depression	any number
Describe	two causes of the Great Depression	2
Research	the "who, what, when, where" of:	
	Herbert Hoover	4
	Franklin Delano Roosevelt	4
	Eleanor Roosevelt	4
Research	the "what, when, where, why" of:	
	Dust Bowl	4
	Great Depression	4
	New Deal	4
	Hoover Dam	4
	Social Security Act of 1935	4
Locate	the region of drought that resulted in the Dust Bowl on a map or globe: Kansas, Texas, New Mexico, Colorado, Nebraska, and Oklahoma	6
	Hoover Dam on a map or globe	1
Graph	the number of people living in the Dust Bowl who were forced to leave	1
Imagine	life before, during, and after the Dust Bowl	3
	life before, during, and after the Great Depression	3
Explain	how grazing and farming made the effects of the drought worse by destroying grass cover	2
	past and present effects of the New Deal	2
	past and present effects of the Depression	2
List	three actions taken under the New Deal	3
	three ways in which the Federal government changed during the New Deal	3
Investigate	WPA (Works Progress Administration) CCC (Civilian Conservation Corps) TVA (Tennessee Valley Authority)	3

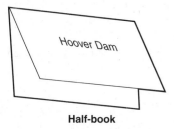

Hoover Dam

Half-book

World War II

Skills/Strategies	Activity Suggestion	Foldable Parts
K-W-L	write about what you know, want to know, and learned about World War II	3
Make a time line	of key events of World War II	any number
Sequence	three events that occurred on December 7, 1941	3
Compare and contrast	World War II before and after United States involvement	2
	democracy and communism	2
List pros and cons	of United States involvement	2
Research	the "who, what, when, where" of:	
	Franklin Delano Roosevelt	4
	Adolf Hitler	4
	Josef Stalin	4
	Benito Mussolini	4
	Winston Churchill	4
	Dwight D. Eisenhower	4
	Harry S. Truman	4
Research	the "what, where, when, why/how" of:	
	Pearl Harbor	4
	atomic bomb	4
	Holocaust	4
	concentration camps	4
	American relocation camps	4
Locate	the following on a map or globe: Pearl Harbor, Island of Oahu, Hawaii Hiroshima, Japan Nagasaki, Japan	any number
Differentiate between	the Axis countries and the Allied countries	2
Make a concept map	of the dictators Hitler, Stalin, and Mussolini	3
	of the Pacific/Asian Front and European Front in World War II	2
	of the Axis countries, Allied countries, Neutral countries in World War II	3
Describe	the American economy before, during, and after the war	3
Outline	arguments for and against the use of relocation camps	2
Research	four battles of World War II	4
List	three effects of World War II on the world	3
Make a Venn diagram	of World War I, World War II, and both	3
Compare	the goals of the United Nations, past and present	2
State	three goals of the United Nations: keep world peace promote justice protect human rights	3

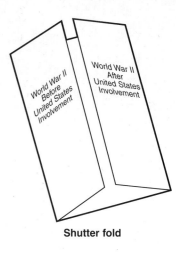

Shutter fold

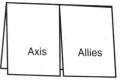

Two-tab book

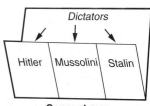

Concept map

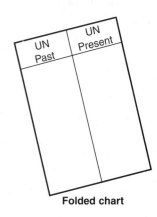

Folded chart

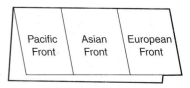

Three-tab book

Cold War

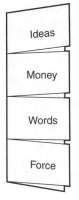

Four-tab book

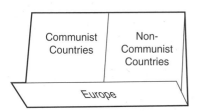

Two-tab matchbook

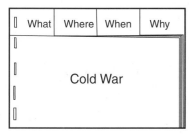

Top-tab book

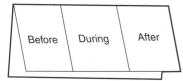

Three-tab book

Skills/Strategies	Activity Suggestion	Foldable Parts
K-W-L	write about what you know, want to know, and learned about the Cold War	3
Make a time line	of key events of the 40-year Cold War	any number
Research	the "who, what, when, where" of:	
	Harry S. Truman	4
	Dwight D. Eisenhower	4
	Joseph McCarthy	4
Research	the "what, where, when, why/how" of:	
	Fair Deal	4
	Cold War	4
	Iron Curtain	4
	NATO, North Atlantic Treaty Organization	4
	Sputnik	4
Locate	the former Soviet Union on a map or globe	1
Explain	how the Cold War was fought with ideas, money, words, and force	4
	what part the space program played in the Cold War	1
Make a concept map	of the two superpowers, United States and Soviet Union	2
Find similarities and differences	between the United States and the Soviet Union	2
List	Europe's communist and noncommunist countries and draw the Iron Curtain between the countries on your list	2
Describe	the effects of the Cold War on the United States and the world	2
	how and why the Cold War ended	2
Show cause and effect	of the arms race	2
	of McCarthyism	2
Summarize	why many Americans feared communism	1
Investigate	Richard Nixon's historic visits to the China (1972) and the Soviet Union (1972) and explain how they eased Cold War tensions	2

Korean War

Skills/Strategies	Activity Suggestion	Foldable Parts
K-W-L	write about what you know, want to know, and learned about the Korean War	3
Research	the "who, what, when,where" of the United Nations, or the UN	4

Locate	on a map or globe:
	   North Korea
	   South Korea
	   Seoul, South Korea's capital city
	   Pyongyang, North Korea's capital city
	   China
		1

Compare and contrast	North Korean and South Korean governments, past and present	4
Investigate	the war on land, air, and sea	3
Research	why the Korean War is said to be one of the bloodiest wars of all time	1
Make a time line	of key events of the Korean War: • June 25, 1950: North Korea invades South Korea; U.N. demands North Korea cease invasion. • June 27, 1950: United States air and naval forces ordered to help defend South Korea. • June 30, 1950: Ground troops sent. • September 8, 1950: Allied troops stop communist advance at Pusan Perimeter. • September 15, 1950: Allied troops land at Inchon. • September 26, 1950: Allies capture Seoul. • October 19, 1950: Allies capture North Korean capital. • October 25, 1950: China supports North Korea. • November 26, 1950: Allies in battle with Chinese. • January 4, 1951: Communists occupy Seoul. • March 14, 1951: Allies reoccupy Seoul. • April 11, 1951: General MacArthur replaced by General Ridgway. • July 10, 1951; Truce talks begin. • April 28, 1952: Communist negotiators reject proposal for voluntary repatriation of prisoners. • October 8, 1952: Truce talks stop. • March 29, 1953: Communists accept UN proposal to exchange sick and wounded prisoners. • April 26, 1953: Truce talks resume. • July 27, 1953: Armistice agreement signed. War ends.	any number

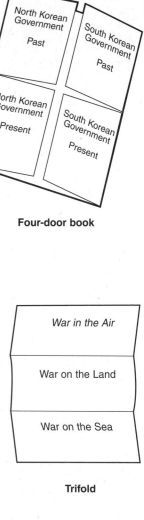

Four-door book

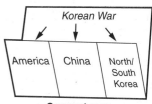

Trifold

Concept map

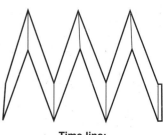

Time line: "Korean War"

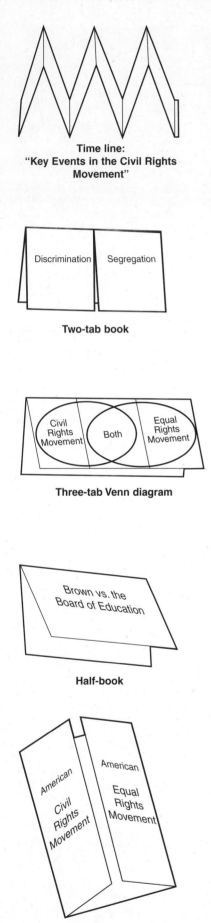

Time line:
"Key Events in the Civil Rights Movement"

Two-tab book

Three-tab Venn diagram

Half-book

Shutter fold

Civil and Equal Rights

Skills/Strategies	Activity Suggestion	Foldable Parts
K-W-L	write about what you know, want to know, and learned about civil and equal rights	3
Make a time line	of key events in the Civil Rights Movement	any number
	of key events in the Equal Rights Movement	any number
Research	the "who, what, when, where" of:	
	Booker T. Washington	4
	Susan B. Anthony	4
	Dr. Martin Luther King, Jr.	4
	Rosa Parks	4
	Thurgood Marshall	4
	Malcolm X	4
	César Chávez and Dolores Huerta	4
Research	the "what, where, when, why" of:	
	The Great Migration	4
	National Association for the Advancement of Colored People, NAACP	4
	Nineteenth Amendment (1920)	4
	League of Women Voters	4
	Watts riots (1965)	4
	La Causa, "The Cause"	4
Define	and give two examples of discrimination	2
	and give two examples of segregation	2
	suffrage	1
Locate	the path of the Great Migration	1
Describe	two things from which African Americans were trying to escape during the Great Migration, poverty and discrimination	2
Show cause and effect	of the increase in African American migration to large cities in the northern United States during World War I	2
compare	civil rights and equal rights	2
Make a Venn diagram	of the Civil Rights Movement, the Equal Rights Movement, and both	3
	of Martin Luther King Jr., César Chávez, and both	3
	of the Civil Rights Act (1964), Voting Rights Act (1965), and both	3
List pros and cons	of demonstrations and marches	2
Discuss	gains made in equal rights for senior citizens, women, and people with disabilities	3
Summarize	Brown versus Board of Education	1
Investigate	the Gray Panthers and Maggie Kuhn	2
Outline	the conception, conditions, and implementation of the Americans with Disabilities Act, or ADA.	3
Research	how President Jimmy Carter helped bring peace between Israel and Egypt and how he made a treaty (SALT II) with the Soviet Union to limit nuclear weapons	2
Show cause and effect	of the Gulf War (1991)	2

Vietnam Era

Skills/Strategies	Activity Suggestion	Foldable Parts
K-W-L	write about what you know, want to know, and learned about the Vietnam Era	3

Locate	on a map or globe:
	   North Vietnam
	   South Vietnam
	   Cambodia
		any number

Research	the "who, what, when, where" of:	
	John F. Kennedy	4
	Lyndon B. Johnson	4
	Richard Nixon	4
Research	the "what, when, where, why/how" of: anti-war protests	4
Analyze	the causes and effects of the Vietnam War	2
Compare and contrast	North Vietnam and South Vietnam before and after the war	4
Make a Venn diagram	of "Hawks," "Doves," and both	3
Explain why	America was bombing North Vietnam and Cambodia	1
Make a time line	of key events of the Vietnam War: • 1957: Viet Cong rebel against South Vietnamese government and Nygo Dinh Diem. • 1963: South Vietnamese generals overthrow the Diem government. • 1964: Congress passes the Tonkin Gulf Resolution. • 1965: President Johnson sends first U.S. ground troops. • 1968: North Vietnam and Viet Cong launches a campaign against South Vietnamese cities. • 1969: President Nixon announces that U.S. troops will begin to withdraw from Vietnam. • 1973: Cease-fire agreement signed. • 1973: U.S. ground troops leave Vietnam. • 1975: South Vietnam surrenders.	any number
Draw and describe	the Vietnam War Memorial	2

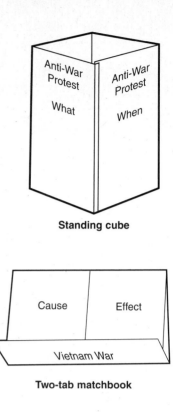

Standing cube

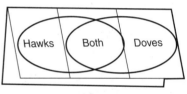

Two-tab matchbook

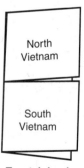

Three-tab Venn diagram

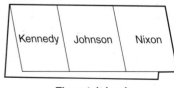

Two-tab book

Three-tab book

Modern Presidents and Policies

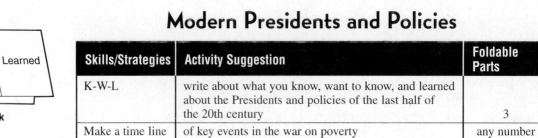

Skills/Strategies	Activity Suggestion	Foldable Parts
K-W-L	write about what you know, want to know, and learned about the Presidents and policies of the last half of the 20th century	3
Make a time line	of key events in the war on poverty	any number
	of the United States space program	any number
	showing key events in the Persian Gulf War	any number
Research	the "who, what, when, where" of Presidents:	
	Dwight D. Eisenhower	4
	John F. Kennedy	4
	Lyndon Baines Johnson	4
	Richard M. Nixon	4
	Gerald R. Ford	4
	James Earl Carter	4
	Ronald W. Reagan	4
	George Bush	4
	William Jefferson Clinton	4
	George W. Bush	4
Research	the "what, where, when, why/how" of:	
	the Peace Corps	4
	Cuban Missile crisis	4
	"Space Race"	4
	Kennedy assassination	4
	"war on poverty"	4
	first moon landing	4
	Watergate scandal	4
	United States bicentennial	4
	Persian Gulf War (1991)	4
	Oklahoma City bombing (1995)	4
	impeachment of President Clinton (1998)	4
Describe	four problems faced by President Kennedy in 1961: the Cold War, arms race with Soviet Union, racial discrimination, and poverty	4
Locate	Cuba on a map and explain what part Fidel Castro has played in the history of Cuba	2
Compare and contrast	the assassinations of John F. Kennedy and Abraham Lincoln	2
Explain	the two things Lyndon Johnson wanted for all Americans, education and health care	2
Outline	four key events in the Watergate scandal	4
Make a concept map	that shows President Nixon's presidency, resignation, and pardon	3

Know	Want to Know	Learned

Three-tab book

Top-tab book

Cold War

Arms Race with Soviet Union

Racial Discrimination

Poverty

Four-tab book

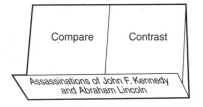

Two-tab matchbook

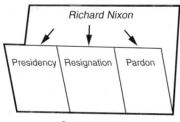

Concept map

The New Millennium

Skills/Strategies	Activity Suggestion	Foldable Parts
K-W-L	write about what you know, want to know, and learned about America entering the 21st century	3

Make a time line	of key events in:
	    the War on Terrorism
	    the history of Afghanistan
	    the history of Israel
	    the history of the Palestinians
		any number

Research	the "who, what, when, where" of:	
	George W. Bush	4
	Tony Blair	4
	Colin Powell	4
	Osama bin Laden	4
Research	the "what, where, when, why/how" of:	
	the war on terrorism	4
	Israeli and Palestinian conflict	4
	Y2K	4
	al Qaeda	4
	Taliban regime	4
Locate	Afghanistan on a map or globe and note two geographic features of the country	2
Compare and contrast	the first years of the 19th, 20th, and 21st centuries	3

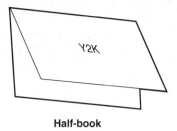

Half-book

Two-tab matchbook

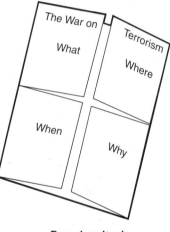

Four-door book

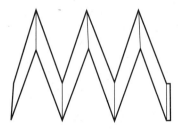

**Time line:
"History of Afghanistan"**

Presidents of the United States

1st	George Washington	(1732–1799)
2nd	John Adams	(1735–1826)
3rd	Thomas Jefferson	(1743–1826)
4th	James Madison	(1751–1836)
5th	James Monroe	(1758–1831)
6th	John Quincy Adams	(1767–1848)
7th	Andrew Jackson	(1767–1845)
8th	Martin Van Buren	(1782–1862)
9th	William Henry Harrison	(1773–1841)
10th	John Tyler	(1790–1862)
11th	James K. Polk	(1795–1849)
12th	Zachary Taylor	(1784–1850)
13th	Millard Fillmore	(1800–1874)
14th	Franklin Pierce	(1804–1869)
15th	James Buchanan	(1791–1868)
16th	Abraham Lincoln	(1809–1865)
17th	Andrew Johnson	(1808–1875)
18th	Ulysses S. Grant	(1822–1885)
19th	Rutherfold B. Hayes	(1822–1893)
20th	James A. Garfield	(1831–1881)
21st	Chester A. Arthur	(1829–1886)
22nd	Grover Cleveland	(1837–1908)
23rd	Benjamin Harrison	(1833–1901)
24th	Grover Cleveland	(1837–1908)
25th	William McKinley	(1843–1901)
26th	Theodore Roosevelt	(1858–1919)
27th	William Howard Taft	(1857–1930)
28th	Woodrow Wilson	(1856–1924)
29th	Warren G. Harding	(1865–1923)
30th	Calvin Coolidge	(1872–1933)
31st	Herbert Hoover	(1874–1964)
32nd	Franklin Delano Roosevelt	(1882–1945)
33rd	Harry S. Truman	(1884–1972)
34th	Dwight D. Eisenhower	(1890–1969)
35th	John F. Kennedy	(1917–1963)
36th	Lyndon Baines Johnson	(1908–1973)
37th	Richard M. Nixon	(1913–1994)
38th	Gerald R. Ford	(1913–)
39th	James Earl Carter	(1924–)
40th	Ronald W. Reagan	(1911–)
41st	George Bush	(1924–)
42nd	William Jefferson Clinton	(1946–)
43rd	George W. Bush	(1946-)

World History

The following social studies topics are covered in this section:

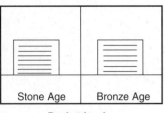

Pocket book

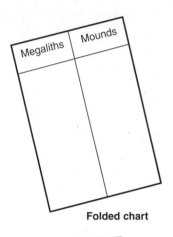

Folded chart

Picture frame book

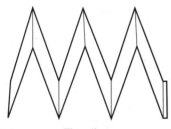

**Time line:
"History of Archaeology"**

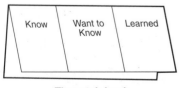

Three-tab book

Skills/Strategies	Activity Suggestion	Foldable Parts
K-W-L	write about what you know, want to know, and learned about early cultures	3
Investigate	the history of archaeology and explain its importance to historians	2
Compare and contrast	past and present techniques used in archaeology	2
Describe	three ways in which technology has changed the way we study archaeological finds	3
Explain	why first interpretations of archaeological findings are not always accurate	1
	the importance of burial sites to our understanding of early cultures and describe why they can provide a wealth of information on early cultures	2
Research	the "what, where, when, why/how" of:	
	Lascaux Caves in France	4
	Stonehenge in England	4
	Silbury Hill in England	4
	Iceman of the Tyrol	4
	Easter Island megaliths	4
Discover	locations in Europe and the Americas where early cultures changed the shape of Earth by moving large amounts of dirt or rock	any number
	two or more megalithic monuments and structures built across Europe	any number
Make a time line	of the history of the domestication of animals	any number
	of the early history of tools and weapons	any number
Compare and contrast	early cultures of foragers to early cultures of food producers	2
	cultures of the Stone Age and cultures of the Bronze Age	2

Fertile Crescent

Pyramid fold

Skills/Strategies	Activity Suggestion	Foldable Parts
K-W-L	write about what you know, want to know, and learned about the history of Mesopotamia and the region called the Fertile Crescent	3
Describe	the land of the Fertile Crescent as desert, rocky mountains, and fertile river bottom	3
Draw and label	the Tigris River, the Euphrates River, and Mesopotamia	3
	rugged mountains and plateaus to the north and fertile plains to the south	2
Explain	what Mesopotamia means and how it got its name	2
	positive and negative effects of floods in this region	2
Make a Venn diagram	of Tigris and Euphrates Rivers, Nile River, and both	3
	of Sumerian King, Egyptian Pharaoh, and both	3
Explain	why a surplus in the southern part of Mesopotamia, called Sumer, resulted in the rise of small cities	1
Make a concept map	of Mesopotamia and its two empires: Sumerian Empire, Babylonian Empire	2
Investigate	the city-states of Sumer before and after they were united under one ruler—Sargon	2
Research	the Code of Hammurabi	1
Make a table	of the achievements of the Mesopotamian civilization: government, religion, architecture, writing	any number
Describe	Mesopotamia in its times of unity and division	2
Outline	the development and use of the wheel	2
	the history of the development of cuneiform writing	any number
Make a table	of the Sumerians, Babylonians, and Israelites, and record information on their writing and records, their government and law, and their type of religion (monotheism or polytheism)	any number
Make a time line	of the history of Judaism	any number
Research	the "who, what, when, where" of:	
	Sargon, king of the city-state Kish	4
	Hammurabi, Babylon's king	4

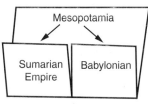

Concept map

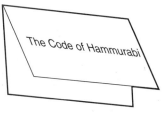

Half-book

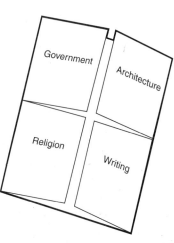

Four-door book

Nile Valley

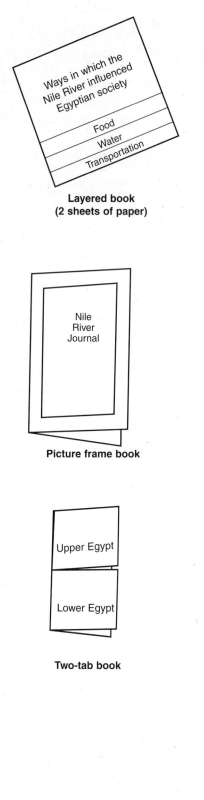

Layered book
(2 sheets of paper)

Picture frame book

Two-tab book

Skills/Strategies	Activity Suggestion	Foldable Parts
K-W-L	write about what you know, want to know, and learned about the Nile Valley	3
Locate	the Nile River on a recent map and the Nile River on a historical map	2
Collect	Nile River facts and trivia in a journal: world's longest river, floods yearly from July to September, has a very rich delta, etc.	any number
Research	the importance of the Nile River to ancient farmers and modern farmers	2
Explain	three ways in which the Nile River influenced Egyptian civilization: provided food, water, and transportation in the middle of a desert	3
	why the Egyptian economy was based upon agriculture and farming	2
Compare and contrast	Upper Egypt and Lower Egypt	2
	achievements made during the Old Kingdom, Middle Kingdom, New Kingdom	3
	Egyptian farms and cities	2
Make a Venn diagram	of land of drought, land of flood, both	3
Investigate	the life of a pharaoh and the impact of the pharaoh on government, religion, and economy	4
Describe	two ways in which Egyptians prepared for the afterlife	2
	the relationship between hieroglyphics, scribes, and papyrus	3
Analyze	how trade and war influenced Egypt during the Middle and New Kingdoms	2
Make a chart	of key events occurring during the Old Kingdom, Middle Kingdom, and New Kingdom	3
Show cause and effect	of Egypt becoming an empire during the New Kingdom	2
Research	Egyptian trade by land and sea	2
Outline	the social structure of Egyptian society: Pharaoh, government officials, soldiers, scribes, merchants, artisans, farmers, and slaves	8
Make a time line	of the history of Ancient Egypt 3500 B.C. to 1100 B.C.	any number
Research	the "what, where, when, how" of:	
	the Rosetta Stone	4
	the Great Pyramid	4
	the Sphinx	4
	the Valley of the Kings	4
Research	the "who, what, when, where" of:	
	a Pharaoh, such as Menes, the first pharaoh, or Tutankhamen	4
	Howard Carter	4

Indus Valley

Skills/Strategies	Activity Suggestion	Foldable Parts
K-W-L	write about what you know, want to know, and learned about the Indus Valley	3
Locate	the Indus River on a map and a globe	2
Trace	the route of the Indus River from its origin in the Himalayas, through deep canyons, desert-like plains, and delta, to where it empties into the Arabian Sea in the Indian Ocean	1
Outline	the history of farming and include information on evidence of early farming in the Indus Valley, 6000 B.C.	any number
Make a Venn diagram	of Indus River, Nile River, and both	3
Compare and contrast	Indus River civilizations, Nile River civilizations, and Tigris-Euphrates River civilizations	3
Investigate	what is known and what is not known about the Harappan civilization of the ancient Indus Valley	2
	the creation of cotton cloth by Harappan workers	1
Explain	why less is known about the Harappan civilization than other civilizations, such as Sumerian	1
Trace	the trade route between Mesopotamia and the Indus Valley	1
Describe	the Aryans, their history, and their migration route	3
Research	how Hinduism grew out of the beliefs of the Aryans	1
Outline	the caste system and its four classes: priests, warriors and rulers, professionals and merchants, and servants	4
Define	reincarnation as a belief in a cycle of life—birth, death, and rebirth	3
Write	about the Four Noble Truths of Buddhism: 1. Life is filled with suffering. 2. Suffering is caused by people's wants. 3. Suffering can be ended if people stop wanting things. 4. To stop wanting things, people must follow eight basic laws.	4
Make a concept map	Buddhism—founder, basic beliefs, basic laws	3
Make a time line	of the history of the Indus Valley	any number
	of the history of Hinduism	any number
	of the history of Buddhism	any number
Research	the "what, when, where, why/how" of: Vedas, or Books of Knowledge	4
Research	the "who, what, when, where" of: Siddhartha Gautama, founder of Buddhism	4

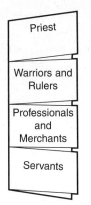

Four-tab book

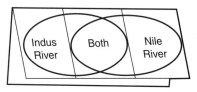

Three-tab Venn diagram

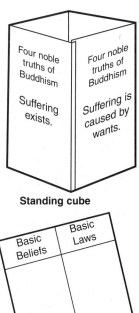

Standing cube

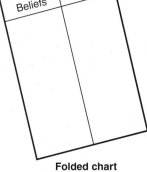

Folded chart

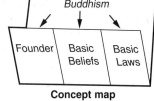

Concept map

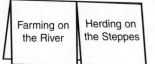

Two-tab book

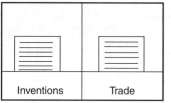

Pocket book

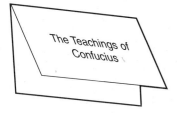

Half-book

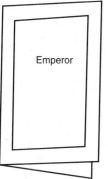

Picture frame book

**Layered book
(2 sheets of paper)**

Huang-He Valley

Skills/Strategies	Activity Suggestion	Foldable Parts
K-W-L	write about what you know, want to know, and learned about the Huang-He Valley	3
Locate	the Huang River, also called the Yellow River, on a map or globe	1
Trace	the route of the Huang River from its beginning on the Tibetan Plateau, through northern China, and note where it empties into the Yellow Sea in the Pacific Ocean	4
Investigate	levees and their use along the Huang River	2
Compare and contrast	two ways of life in ancient China—farming along the river and herding on the steppes	2
Research	the Shang dynasty, its development in the Huang River delta, and its rule from 1700 B.C. to 1100 B.C.	3
	inventions and technology of ancient China	2
Describe	three of the teachings of Confucius	3
Chart	the advances made during the 400-year Han dynasty in science, mathematics, the arts, and trade	any number
Show the effects	of Confucianism on life during the Han dynasty	any number
Make a time line	of the history of Ancient China	any number
	of the history of Chinese writing	any number
	of the history of silk	any number
Research	the "what, when, where, why/ how" of: the Great Wall of China	4
Research	the "who, what, when, where" of: the mummy of Fu Hao, a woman found in a royal tomb in Anyang	4

Ancient Greece

Skills/Strategies	Activity Suggestion	Foldable Parts
K-W-L	write about what you know, want to know, and learned about Ancient Greece	3
Locate	Ancient Greece on a historical map and modern Greece on a political map	2
Describe	three geographical features of Ancient Greece: rocky peninsulas, islands, and good harbors	3
Show effects	of the Aegean sea on life in Ancient Greece	1
	of the climate on farming in Ancient Greece	1
Investigate	the islands of Crete and Rhodes	2
Draw maps of	a Greek city-state, its agora, and its acropolis	3
Explain	the importance of the Mediterranean Sea for trade and the transfer of culture	2
	how the Greeks obtained slaves through war, debt, and piracy	3
Research	the history of the production of olive oil	any number
List	products that were imported and products that were exported	2
Compare and contrast	life in the city-states of Sparta and Athens	2
	citizenship in Ancient Greece to citizenship in the United States	2
	the Olympic Games, past and present	2
Make a table	outlining the government, daily life, and attitudes of the people in the city-states of Sparta and Athens	2
List pros and cons	of the expansion of Greek culture and the Greek empire	2
Discover	what is known about Alexandria's museum, library, and lighthouse	3
Make a time line	of the history of Ancient Greece	any number
	on the history of the Olympic Games	any number
Research	the "what, when, where, why/how" of:	
	Acropolis	4
	Athen's Golden Age	4
	Parthenon	4
Research	the "who, what, when, where" of:	
	Socrates	4
	Plato	4
	Aristotle	4
	Alexander the Great	4

**Layered book
(2 sheets of paper)**

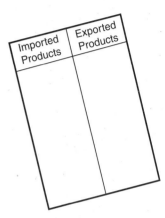

Folded chart

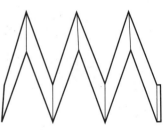

**Time line:
"Olympic Games"**

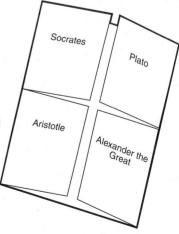

Four-door book

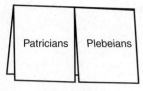

Two-tab book

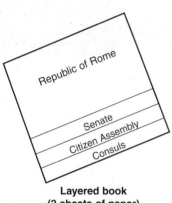

**Layered book
(2 sheets of paper)**

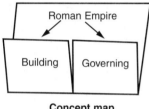

Concept map

**Time line:
"History of the Roman Empire"**

Picture frame book

Ancient Rome

Skills/Strategies	Activity Suggestion	Foldable Parts
K-W-L	write about what you know, want to know, and learned about Ancient Rome	3
Locate	Ancient Rome on a historical map and modern Rome on a political map	2
Note	the geography of Italy—mountains and plains—and research the Alps, the Apennine Mountains, and the Latium Plain	3
Describe	the geography of Ancient Rome and how it contributed to the development of Roman culture	2
Research	the Etruscans and explain how they created a unified Italy	2
Tell	the legend of Romulus and Remus and the founding of Rome	1
Compare and contrast	government in Ancient Rome before and after it became a republic	2
	views of the patricians and the plebeians	2
Explain	why Rome is called the City of Seven Hills	1
	the three branches of the Republic of Rome—senate, the citizen assembly, and the consuls	3
Show cause and effect	of the Punic Wars and the defeat of Carthage	2
List	three examples of Roman contributions to the world	3
Describe	the period in Roman history called Pax Romana	1
Outline	the rise and spread of Christianity during the Pax Romana	2
	how troubles within and outside the Roman Empire lead to the decline of the Roman Empire	2
	the rise and fall of the Roman Empire	2
Make a concept map	of the Roman Empire—building an empire and governing an empire	2
	of Rome—eastern and western empires	2
Make a chart	of ways in which Ancient Rome influenced the world through government, architecture, and language	3
Make a time line	of the history of the Roman Empire	any number
Research	the "what, when, where, why/how" of:	
	Colosseum	4
	Pantheon	4
Research	the "who, what, when, where" of:	
	Julius Caesar	4
	Cleopatra	4
	Augustus	4
	gladiators	4

Ancient Americas

Skills/Strategies	Activity Suggestion	Foldable Parts
K-W-L	write about what you know, want to know, and learned about Ancient Americas	3
Locate	the prehistoric land bridge, Beringia, and the current Bering Strait	2
Make a Venn diagram	of Beringia, Bering Strait, and both	3
Research	the geography and climate of North America, Middle America, and South America	3
Outline	how people might have first come to the Americas	any number
Explain	two reasons why people might migrate from one area to another: climate, hunting, escape enemies, etc.	2
Investigate	the Olmec civilization	3 or more
Identify and describe	three or more achievements of the Olmec	3 or more
	three or more achievements of the Maya	3 or more
	three achievements of the Aztec	3 or more
	three achievements of the Inca	3 or more
Investigate	the importance of astronomy to the Maya	1
Make a concept map	of Middle American civilizations: Olmec, Maya, and Aztec	3
Make a time line	of the history of Middle America	any number
Research	the "what, when, where, why/how" of:	
	the Ice Age	4
	Chichén Itzá	4
	Mexico	4
	La Venta, Mexico	4
	Copán, Mexico	4

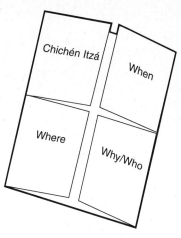

Four-door book

Standing cube

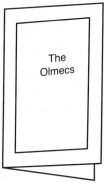

Picture frame book

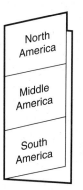

Three-tab book

The Arab World

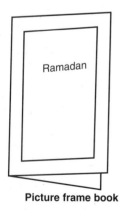

Time line:
"History of Islam"

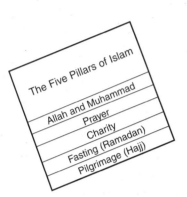

Folded book
(3 sheets of paper)

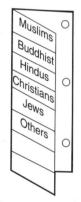

Vocabulary book

Skills/Strategies	Activity Suggestion	Foldable Parts
K-W-L	write about what you know, want to know, and learned about the Arab World	3
Locate	Arabia on a map and globe	2
Define	peninsula and describe Arabia as a peninsula	2
Show cause and effect	of desert land and desert oasis	2
Trace	trade routes linking Arabia with Egypt and the Fertile Crescent on a map	any number
Research	The Five Pillars of Islam	5
	the sacred month of Ramadan	1
Describe	what you think would happen before, during, and after a pilgrimage	3
Explain	how the spread of the Islamic empire enriched and was enriched by other civilizations	2
	caliph, caliphate, Baghdad	3
Make a Venn diagram	of the Roman Empire, Islamic Empire, and both	3
Compare and contrast	the beliefs of any two religions: Muslims, Buddhists, Hindus, Christians, Jews, and others	2
Make a chart	showing the achievements of the Caliphate in: medicine, math and science, architecture, and literature	4
Make a time line	of the history of Islam	any number
Research	the "what, when, where, why or how" of:	
	Mecca	4
	Kaaba	4
	Quran	4
Research	the "who, what, when, where" of Muhammad	4

Ramadan

Picture frame book

African Civilizations

Skills/Strategies	Activity Suggestion	Foldable Parts
K-W-L	write about what you know, want to know, and learned about African civilizations	3
Locate	ancient African civilizations on a historic map and note what countries are currently located in these regions on a political map	2
Investigate	Africa's mountains, rivers, deserts, grasslands, and forests	5
	Africa's population, economy, and governments	3
Compare and contrast	Saharan Africa and Subsaharan Africa, past and present	4
Explain	why Africa is often said to be "The Cradle of Civilization"	1
Make a Venn diagram	of Kush, Ancient Egypt, and both	3
Describe	empires and the known history of Northwest Africa, West Africa, East Africa, and South Africa	4
Compare	Mombasa, Zanzibar, and Mogadishu, past and present	6
Show cause and effect	of trade in ivory and gold	2
Search the web	for information on early civilizations in Great Zimbabwe	any number
Make a chart	of Africa's Eastern Coast—location, resources, needs and wants, a trade	4
Make a table	showing the accomplishments of the independent kingdoms of Kush, Aksum, and Zagwe in northeastern Africa	3
Make a concept map	of western empires rich in rold—Ghana, Mali, and Songhai	3
Make a time line	of the history of Africa	any number
Research	the "what, when, where, why/how" of:	
	Rock Churches of Lalibela, Ethiopia	4
	Timbuktu	4
Research	the "who, what, when, where" of:	
	King Mansa	4
	Musa	4

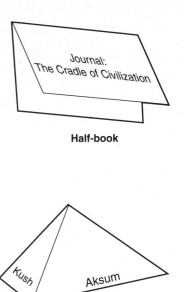

Half-book

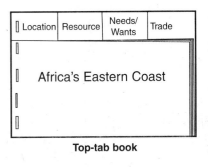

Pyramid fold

Top-tab book

Three-tab book

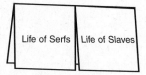

Two-tab book

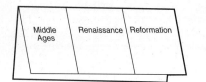

Three-tab book

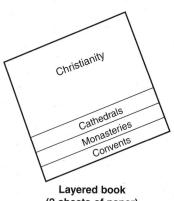

**Layered book
(2 sheets of paper)**

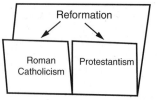

Concept map

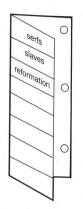

Vocabulary book

The Middle Ages and the Renaissance

Skills/Strategies	Activity Suggestion	Foldable Parts
K-W-L	write about what you know, want to know, and learned about Europe in transition	3
Locate	Europe on a map and globe and investigate the countries that comprise this continent	2
Investigate	three or more geographic features of Europe: long coastlines and good harbors, mountains, farm land, navigable rivers, temperate climate	3 or more
Compare and Contrast	the land and water of Europe and the land and water of Africa	4
	the Middle Ages and the Renaissance	2
Find similarities and differences	between serfs and slaves	2
Show cause and effect	of the growth of towns and trade	2
Describe	some aspects of Christianity during this time: cathedrals, monasteries, convents	3
Outline	the history of the Crusades	any number
Explain	the relations between the Christians and the Jews in Europe at this time	2
	how the Renaissance was a mixture of old and new knowledge	2
Write	about an imaginary pilgrimage	1
Research	the cause and effect of the Black Death	2
Make a chart	on the accomplishments of the Middle Ages and the Renaissance	2
	on information on the Middle Ages, the Renaissance, and the Reformation	3
Make a concept map	about manors—serfs, knights, vassals, lord and lady	4
	about the Christian Church, divided into the Eastern Orthodox Church and the Roman Catholic Church	2
	about how the Reformation altered Roman Catholicism and created Protestantism	2
Make a time line	of the history of Europe	any number
Research	the "what, when, where, why/how" of:	
	the Magna Carta, 1215	4
	the Norman Invasion	4
Research	the "who, what, when, where" of:	
	Charlemagne	4
	William the Conqueror	4
	King John I	4
	Leonardo da Vinci	4
	Nicolaus Copernicus	4
	Martin Luther	4
	Queen Elizabeth I of England	4

New Empires in Asia

Skills/Strategies	Activity Suggestion	Foldable Parts
K-W-L	write about what you know, want to know, and learned about new empires in Asia	3
Find	Asia on a map and globe and investigate the countries that comprise this continent	2
Research	the six regions of Asia: North, West, Central, South, Southeast, and East	6
	the travels of Marco Polo	any number
Investigate	three or more geographic features of Asia: size, coastlines, mountain ranges, deserts, grasslands, arctic regions	3 or more
	how mountains affect life in positive and negative ways on this continent	2
	China's Forbidden City	1
Compare and contrast	the land and water of Asia and the land and water of Europe	2
	Hinduism and Buddhism	2
Make a concept map	showing Eurasia as one giant continent composed of Europe and Asia	2
Determine	what separates Asia from Europe and Africa	1
Define	monsoon, archipelago, plateau, peninsula	4
Research	the "what, when, where, why/how" of:	
	the Ottoman Empire	4
	the Mogul Empire	4
	Khmer Kingdom of Southeast Asia	4
	Ming dynasty of China	4
	the Silk Road	4
Research	the "who, what, when, where" of:	
	Sultan, Süleyman, Ottoman Empire	4
	Akbar, Mogul ruler	4
	Genghis Khan and/or Kublai Khan	4
	Marco Polo, explorer	4
	Yoritomo, first Japanese shogun	4
Locate	10 countries in Asia on a map or globe, and find their largest cities	10
Describe	feudal Japan	1
Make a concept map	of the Japanese feudal system, composed of shoguns, lords, farmers, and samurai	4
Make a time line	of the history of the Ottoman Empire	any number
	of the history of the Mogul Empire	any number
	of the Khmer Kingdom	any number
	of China's Ming dynasty	any number
Research	life in Japan between 1603 and 1867	any number
Make a table	about countries, dynasties, rulers, capital cities, achievements	5

Half-book

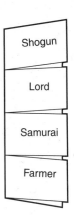

Four-tab book

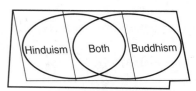

Three-tab Venn diagram

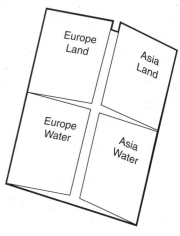

Four-door book

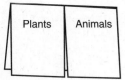

Plants | Animals

Two-tab book

Geography of America	
Size	
Coastline	
Mountain Ranges	
Deserts	
Grasslands	
Forests	
Tundra Regions	
Vocabulary Words	

Layer book
(8 sheets of paper)

North America

South America

Two tab book

Empire	Location	Culture	Achievement
Aztec			
Inca			
Maya			

4x4 Folded table

New Empires in the Americas

Skills/Strategies	Activity Suggestion	Foldable Parts
K-W-L	write about what you know, want to know, and learned about the empires in the Americas	3
Find	North and South America on a map and globe and investigate the countries that comprise this continent	any number
Describe	common plants and animals of the Americas from north to south	any number
	the different climate zones from north to south	any number
Investigate	three geographic features of the Americas: size, coastlines, mountain ranges, deserts, grasslands, forests, or tundra regions	3
	how mountains have affected the growth of civilization	1
Define	tundra, timberline, isthmus, chinampas, terrace, quipu	6
Make a Venn diagram	of the Andes, the Rockies, and both	3
	of the Aztec empire, Egyptian kingdom, and both	3
	of the Inca empire, Aztec empire, and both	3
Explain	how the Great Lakes formed	1
Locate	on a map or globe: Canadian Shield the Rocky Mountains the Andes Mountains Isthmus of Panama Mexico City Cuzco Machu Picchu	any number
Research	the "what, where, when, why/how" of:	
	the Great Plaza at Tenochtitlián	4
	the fall of the Aztec civilization	4
Make a table	about empire, location, culture, important rulers, and known achievements	5
Make a concept map	about the triple alliance formed by Tenochtitlán, Texcoco, and Tlacopan	3
Make a time line	of the history of the Aztec empire	any number
	of the history of the Inca empire	any number
	of the Ojibwa people of North America	any number
Research	the Ice Ages	1
	peoples of the Andes, past and present	2
	three groups of early people of North America: Ojibwa, Ottawa, Cree, Huron, Menominee, and others	3
Describe	the form and function of the Aztec pyramids	2
Compare and contrast	agriculture in the Aztec city of Tenochtitlán and agriculture in mountainous Inca cities	2
	the road system of the Inca Empire and the road system of the Roman Empire	2

Europe Explores and Expands

Skills/Strategies	Activity Suggestion	Foldable Parts
K-W-L	write about what you know, want to know, and learned about European expansion, which began in the late 1400s	3
Research	advances in sailing technologies during this time, such as the design of the caravel	any number
Show cause and effect	of advances in sailing technologies and the beginning of an age of exploration	2
	of Spain's conquest of the empires of America	2
List pros and cons	of exploration and expansion	2
Define	caravel, strait, conquistador, missionary, convert	5
Research	the "who, what, when where" of:	
	Prince Henry of Portugal	4
	Bartholomeu Dias	4
	Moctezuma	4
	Francisco Pizarro	4
	Atahualpa, emperor of Inca empire	4
	James Cook	4
Research	the "what, where, when, why/how" of: the Line of Demarcation	4
Make a chart	of explorers, their lives, achievements, and adventures	4
Make a table	of explorers, dates, routes, and discoveries	4
Make a time line	of the history of exploration by sea	any number
	of European exploration of the Americas	any number
	of the development of slavery in the Americas	any number
Explain	why Europeans wanted to find a cheaper route to Asia	1
List	five difficulties faced by early explorers	5
	three difficulties faced by a nation ruling distant lands	3
Compare and contrast	past and present attitudes towards nations taking the land of another nation	2
	American land claimed by Spain and American land claimed by Portugal in the year 1600	2
Research	the Line of Demarcation, drawn in 1494	1
	and explain the triangular trade route between the West Indies, Africa, and Europe: trade of sugar, European goods, and slaves	3
Describe	how life for the conquered people in the Americas was shaped by missionaries, mining, and farm work	3
Discover	two important reasons for the English colonization of Australia	2

Picture frame book

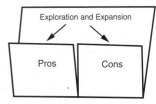

4x4 folded table

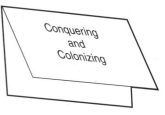

Concept map

Half-book

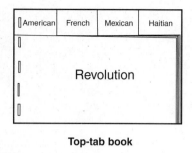

Top-tab book

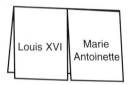

Pyramid

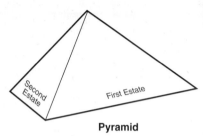

Two-tab book

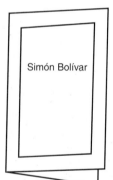

Picture frame book

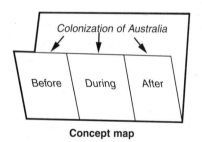

Concept map

Revolution and Change

Skills/Strategies	Activity Suggestion	Foldable Parts
K-W-L	write about what you know, want to know, and learned about how revolutions and expansionism changed the world from the late 1700s to the late 1600s	3
Find	France on a map or globe and note three geographic features	3
Describe	France's Age of Discontent	1
	the three estates, or social classes, of France in 1789: First Estate, Catholic clergy Second Estate, aristocracy Third Estate, all other people	3
Investigate	two conditions leading to the French Revolution	2
Research	"Declaration of the Rights of Man and of the Citizen"	1
Research	the "what, where, when, why/how" of:	
	the Reign of Terror	4
	the French Revolution	4
	the American Revolution	4
Research	the "who, what, when, where" of:	
	Louis XVI	4
	Marie Antoinette	4
	Maximilien Robespierre	4
	Napoleon Bonaparte	4
	Miguel Hidalgo	4
	Simón Bolívar and José de San Martín	4
Note	similarities and differences between the French and American revolutions	2
Define	monarchy, divine right, revolution, peasants, factory	5
Make a Venn diagram	of revolution in the Caribbean, revolution in Mexico, and both	3
	of the United States, Haiti, and both	3
Explain	how the Great Lakes formed	1
Research	and locate on a map or globe, colonized lands in the 1700s, 1800s, and 1900s	3
Make a chart	of three revolutionary leaders and their characteristics	3
Make a table	of colonies, date of colonization, colonizing country, date of independence, leaders of independence	any number
Make a concept map	of Mexico, before, during, and after colonization	3
Make a time line	of the history of Australia before, during, and after colonization	any number
	of a country's struggle for independence	any number
Find similarities and differences	between the French Revolution or American Revolution and the Industsrial Revolution	2
List	positive and negative effects of revolution	2
Investigate	Japan before and after 1854 when it became open to world trade	2
Summarize	Commodore Perry's role in Japan's history	1
Outline	the expansion of Japan	any number

Troubled World

Skills/Strategies	Activity Suggestion	Foldable Parts
K-W-L	write about what you know, want to know, and learned about the world during times of trouble	3
Research	inflation and depression and explain how they affect the world economy	2
Cause and effect	of strong feelings of nationalism prior to World War I	2
List	Allies and Central Powers of World War I	2
	Allies and Axis Powers of World War II	2
Define	nationalism, alliance, armistice, communism, strike, totalitarian, tsar, fascism, inflation, depression, propaganda, concentration camp	12
Locate	on a map or globe: 　Sarajevo 　Serbia 　Austria-Hungary 　Russia	any number
Research	the "who, what, when, where" of:	
	Archduke Franz Ferdinand	4
	Alexander II	4
	Nicholas II	4
	Vladimir Ilyich Lenin	4
	Josef Stalin	4
	Adolf Hitler	4
Research	the "what, when, where, when" of:	
	Bloody Sunday (1905)	4
	Allied Powers	4
	Central Powers	4
	League of Nations	4
	Treaty of Versailles	4
	Axis Powers	4
	Holocaust	4
Explain	how World War I and World War II started	2
Compare and contrast	the Russian Revolution and the triumph of communism in China	2
Describe	the results of World War I and World War II	2
	the Russian Revolution (1917–1920)	1
	the Cultural Revolution in China (1966–1976)	1
Make a chart	of events of World War I, Russian Revolution, World War II, and communism in China	any number
Make a table	describing war/revolution, date, cause, result	any number
Make a concept map	about technology as it relates to World War I and World War II	2
Make a time line	of the key events in the following: 　World War I and World War II, and the revolutions 　in Russia and China	any number
Outline	the growth of Russia from 1300s to early 1900s	1
Show the causes and effects	of the Cold War	2
Explain	how foreign rule and imperial rule ended in China	2

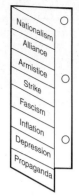

Vocabulary book

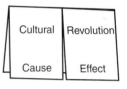

Two-tab book

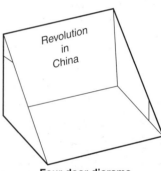

Four-door diorama

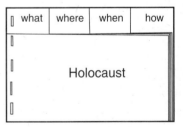

Top-tab book

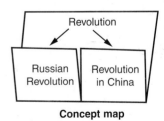

Concept map

The Spread of Independence

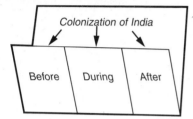

Top-tab book

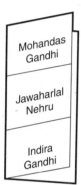

Concept map

Mohandas
Gandhi

Jawaharlal
Nehru

Indira
Gandhi

**Three-tab book
(vertical)**

African Colonies	Date of Colonization	Date of Independence	Important Events or People
colony			
colony			
colony			

4x4 folded table

Skills/Strategies	Activity Suggestion	Foldable Parts
K-W-L	write about what you know, want to know, and learned about the spread of independence around the world	3
Explain	how three countries in Africa gained independence from European rule	3
Locate	on a map or globe: 　Accra 　Ghana 　Egypt 　Suez Canal 　Middle Eastern countries 　Southeast Asian countries	any number
Define	nationalism, boycott, independence, refugees	4
Explain	two effects of European colonialism on Africa	2
	why more than 100 nations have gained independence since 1943	1
Research	the "who, what, when, where" of:	
	Kwame Nkrumah	4
	Gamal Abdel Nasser	4
	Mohandas Gandhi	4
	Ho Chi Minh	4
Research	the "what, where, when, why" of:	
	Palestine Liberation Organization, PLO	4
	Zionism	4
	Vietnam War (1954–1975)	4
Make a chart	of the 14 countries in the Middle East and use it to collect information on each country	14
Make a table	of African colonies, date of colonization, date of independence, and important events or people	any number
Make a concept map	India before, during, and after colonization	3
Describe	how Southeast Asia's independence resulted in Vietnam, Laos, and Cambodia	3
Make a time line	of the history of colonization of Africa	any number
	of the Israeli-Palestinian conflict	any number
	of the Jewish struggle for a homeland	any number
Sequence	the events leading to India's independence	any number
List	three changes that the British East India Company brought to the Indian subcontinent	3
Investigate	the lives of Mohandas Gandhi, Jawaharlal Nehru, and Indira Gandhi	3
Research	how the nations in Southeast Asia gained independence from France, Britain, and the Netherlands	3

A Changing World

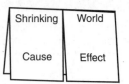

Two-tab book

Skills/Strategies	Activity Suggestion	Foldable Parts
K-W-L	write about what you know, want to know, and learned about the changing world in which we live	3
Discuss	how and why the world is "shrinking"	2
Define	ethnic groups and apartheid	2
Describe	how the end of the Cold War changed the political and economic state of Eastern Europe	2
	three ways in which the "information revolution" links people around the world	3
	how South Africans achieved democracy	1
Research	the "who, what, when, where" of:	
	Mikhail Gorbachev	4
	Ronald Reagan	4
	Lech Walesa	4
	Boris Yeltsin	4
	Nelson Mandela	4
	Frederik Willem de Klerk	4
Research	the "what, where, when, why/how" of:	
	Tiananmen Square, 1989	4
	Nunavut Territory, April 1, 1999	4
	NAFTA, North American Free Trade Agreement, 1993	4
	apartheid	4
	"Year of Miracles" in Europe, 1989	4

Locate	on a map or globe:
	    Yugoslavia
	    Balkan Peninsula
	    Former Soviet Union
	    South Africa
	    Hong Kong
	    the Pacific Rim
		any number

Make a chart	of information about the Soviet Union, before and after 1991	any number
Make a concept map	about how Czechoslovakia became two separate nations: Czech Republic and Slovakia	2
Make a time line	of the history of Hong Kong	any number
	of the history of Quebec	any number
Research	two things that replaced the tension of the Cold War: conflicts over nationalism and ethnic differences	2
Summarize	how life in Eastern Europe, Russia, China, and the Americas has changed since World War II	4
Compare and contrast	South American nations with democracies and nations with dictatorships	2
List pros and cons	of the European Union	2

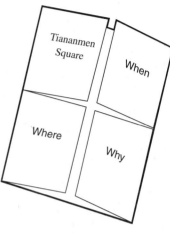

Four-door book

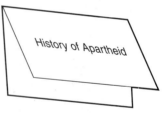

Half-book

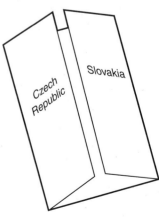

Shutter fold

Index